Living Hymn Stories

Wilbur Konkel

BETHANY HOUSE PUBLISHERS
MINNEAPOLIS, MINNESOTA 55438
A Division of Bethany Fellowship, Inc.

OTHER BOOKS BY WILBUR KONKEL

Stories of Children's Hymns
More Living Hymn Stories
Amazing Grace Hymn Stories
Jungle Gold

Some of the stories
from *Stories of Children's Hymns*
have been incorporated
into this edition.

Living Hymn Stories
Wilbur Konkel

Library of Congress Catalog Card Number 82-072557

ISBN 0-87123-317-7

Published by Bethany House Publishers
A Division of Bethany Fellowship, Inc.
6820 Auto Club Road, Minneapolis, Minnesota 55438

Printed in the United States of America

Foreword

I appreciate tremendously the work Wilbur Konkel is doing. He is making the hymns live as he writes and publishes their stories. I sincerely trust that *Living Hymn Stories* will prove a great blessing to those who read them, and that the hymns will mean more than ever before because of these living stories.

Dr. Oswald J. Smith

The Author

WILBUR KONKEL, D. D. is Director for West African Missions of the Pillar of Fire Church. He attended Denver University and Bellview College before he was called to the ministry. He earned a degree at Christ College, Oxford, and has served as a minister in Great Britain for 20 years. He now lives in Colorado.

Introduction

What a delight it has been gathering the information for this fourth volume of hymn stories! My information has been culled from many sources. I have tried to acknowledge authors from whom I have quoted. If any have been overlooked, forgive me.

I wish to express my appreciation to Dr. Oswald Smith, world renowned missionary statesman, author, hymnwriter and faithful minister of the everlasting Gospel of the saving grace of our Lord and Saviour, Jesus Christ. His hymns have been a great inspiration to me. I am indebted to Dr. Smith for his foreword to *Living Hymn Stories*.

I also wish to express appreciation to The Rodeheaver Company for permission to quote the words of "Living for Jesus." It was this hymn that inspired the title of this book, *Living Hymn Stories*.

My friend, Rev. John Kelly, has typed my manuscript for which I am grateful.

To all who love to sing of my Redeemer, and who are living for Jesus, I dedicate *Living Hymn Stories*.

Wilbur Konkel

Contents

Living for Jesus

In Philippians 1:21 St. Paul said, "For me to live is Christ." This is living! Life without Him is death. Trying to live without Jesus is like a dying man entering a race. It is hopeless. Jesus said, "Without me ye can do nothing." The hymn writer T. O. Chisholm had this thought in mind when he was sent a hymn tune by his composer friend C. Harold Lowden. Mr. Lowden, who left a successful post as an insurance salesman to become a composer of sacred music, had composed a tune which he felt the Lord had given him. He had put words to the music but did not feel his own words were worthy of the tune the Lord Himself had given. When the Rev. T. O. Chisholm heard the tune it seemed to suggest a full and complete consecration to the Lord Jesus Christ. With the words of St. Paul in mind, "For me to live is Christ," he wrote the words of that lovely consecration hymn:

Living for Jesus, a life that is true:
Trying to please Him in all that I do;
Yielding allegiance glad-hearted and free;
This is the pathway of blessing for me.*

When I was in high school and later in law school, this hymn had a great influence on me. I would feel the Lord calling me, and I so wanted to respond. I would resolve to do better, to live for Jesus, but something always hindered me. I did not know what, but something always seemed to trip me up every time I tried to please Him.

* Words and music copyright the Rodeheaver Co. Used by permission.

It was that third line. My allegiance was to another, and I was not free. My allegiance was to
the powers of darkness and I was bound and
fettered with my own sins. When I heard this
hymn sung in church, as it often was, I resolved
to do better, to start living for some purpose;
to live for Jesus.

> O Jesus, Lord and Saviour,
> I give myself to Thee;
> For Thou in Thine atonement
> Didst give Thyself for me.
> I own no other Master;
> My heart shall be Thy throne;
> My life I give, henceforth to live,
> O Christ, for Thee alone.

Then came the moment in my life when I had
to choose between a law career, fulfilling my own
selfish ambitions, or following Christ. He must
be my Lord and Master or I must continue to
follow the path that leads to destruction. I could
not serve God and sin. I wanted both. I wanted
to follow a law career, make plenty of money
and then serve the Lord on weekends. The Lord
wanted my life, my all, my ambitions and my
failures. When I was finally able to say, "My
life I give, henceforth to live, O Christ, for Thee
alone," the sunshine of heaven flooded my heart.
For the first time in my life I was "glad-hearted
and free." From my heart I sing, "This is the
pathway of blessing for me."

The Rev. T. O. Chisholm, who wrote these
lovely words, was the author of two or three
other hymns that will always be loved wherever
the name of Jesus is mentioned. He was the author
of "Great Is Thy Faithfulness," taking his theme
from the Lamentations of Jeremiah. He wrote
"The Prodigal Son," after his conversion. Out in
Franklin, Kansas, young Chisholm had attended

a series of revival meetings conducted by the Rev. Dr. H. C. Morrison. The Rev. Morrison had preached on the text "Except a man be born again he cannot see the kingdom of God." (John 3:3). In his poem, young Chisholm wanted to stress the fact that the young man had to confess his sins, leave his life of evil, and go "back to my Father and home." The composer, George C. Stebbins, put the words to music, and rarely has it been sung in revival meetings without some prodigal finding Christ.

The Rev. T. O. Chisholm found his health failing and felt the pressures of the ministry too much for him, so he went into the insurance business. What a coincidence that C. Harold Lowden, who left a career as an insurance agent, to devote his time to sacred music and spiritual things, would call on a minister, who, because of poor health, was selling insurance. Mr. Lowden said he simply kept himself ready and listened for God to speak. He wrote the music as the Lord sang it in his heart. Mr. Chisholm got his inspiration from the Bible, usually taking his theme from some Scripture text. No wonder we have this most beautiful hymn.

> Living for Jesus who died in my place,
> Bearing on Calvary my sin and disgrace.
> Such love constrains me to answer His call,
> Follow His leading and give Him my all.

On one occasion I attended a murder trial. A young man was accused of shooting his father in cold blood. It was brought out that he had been provoked beyond endurance by his drunken father repeatedly molesting and beating his mother. The judge decreed that there were no mitigating circumstances in his case and pronounced the young man guilty. His mother, brokenhearted,

cried out for leniency for her son. She cried,
"Punish me, but not my son." Poor mother, she
could not die in her son's place. He had to bear
the penalty for his sins. Jesus did suffer for our
sins, and theirs, bearing on Calvary our sin and
disgrace. Such love constrains me to answer His
call, follow His leading, and give Him my all.

> Living for Jesus, wherever I am
> Doing each duty in His holy name,
> Willing to suffer affliction and loss,
> Deeming each trial a part of my cross.

Some people quote the proverb, "When in
Rome do as the Romans do" and change its meaning to a spiritual application. It was godlessness
and immoral pleasure that brought about the fall
of Rome. Living for Jesus, in Rome or at home,
should be the purpose of every born-again Christian. Living for Jesus wherever I am.

> Living for Jesus thro' earth's little while
> My dearest treasure, the light of His smile
> Seeking the lost ones He died to redeem,
> Bringing the weary to find rest in Him.

Seeking the lost ones He died to redeem, is
our great commission. Indeed it is our greatest
joy. Praying with a taxi driver in Africa, who
wanted Jesus Christ as his Saviour, or with a
young man on the street in Oakland was to me
a great pleasure. Our raison d'etre is to bring
Christ to the lost, or to bring the lost to Him.
This is sufficient reason for an organized church.

What is your purpose in life? Are you seeking the things of this world that are soon to be
lost forever? Is making a living your chief purpose in life? That is important, but should be
secondary. Move up to the cross, find Christ as

your Saviour, then your heart will sing:

> O Jesus, Lord and Saviour,
> I give myself to Thee,
> For Thou in Thy atonement,
> Didst give Thyself for me.
> I own no other Master,
> My heart shall be Thy throne,
> My life I give, henceforth to live,
> O Christ, for Thee alone.

All the Way My Saviour Leads Me

The doctor made a mistake. A little mistake can turn out to be a disaster. That is what happened in the case of the blind hymn writer Fanny Crosby. The doctor put the wrong drops in her eyes when she was only six weeks old, causing her to be blind the rest of her life. Did I say it was a mistake, a disaster? The saintly hymn writer said it differently. She said it was God's will for her. "I verily believe," she said, "that it was God's intention that I should live my days in physical darkness so to be better prepared to sing His praise and to incite others to do so. I could not have written the thousands of hymns if I had been hindered by the distractions that would have been presented to my notice." Can it be that God has a plan for your life, even in spite of your physical problems? Could it be that those physical problems are part of His plan to make you a tower of strength for Him? From the time she was an infant Fanny Crosby was physically blind. She was dependent on others to lead her, to show her the way. How fitting then that she could sing:

All the way my Saviour leads me;
What have I to ask beside?
Can I doubt His tender mercy
Who through life has been my Guide?
Heavenly peace, divinest comfort,
Here by faith in Him to dwell!
For I know whate'er befall me,
Jesus doeth all things well;
For I know whate'er befall me,
Jesus doeth all things well.

She who was physically blind needed a dependable and friendly seeing guide. Yet she who could see a "spring of joy" had a loving and faultless Guide. Her sightless journey would soon be over. In a few short years she would see her Saviour face to face. How fitting then for her to say: "All the way my Saviour leads me; what have I to ask beside? Can I doubt His tender mercy, Who through life has been my Guide?" Yes, blessed assurance, Jesus doeth all things well!

"Who through life has been my Guide"
so wrote Fanny Crosby.

"Our Guide even unto death"
sang King David. The King of Israel had a Royal Guide. He tells us: "For this God is our God for ever and ever; He will be our Guide even unto death." This is not the first time the king had mentioned the fact. Many years before he had said: "He leadeth me." He leadeth me. Those comforting and assuring words have been a blessing to countless thousands. "He leadeth me beside the still waters. He leadeth me in the paths of righteousness for His name's sake." One thing that people and sheep have in common is that they go astray without a Guide. But how can I be sure the Lord will guide me as he did King David and Fanny Crosby? I can trust His word.

We have His promise. "I will instruct thee and teach thee in the way which thou shalt go: I will guide thee with mine eye." (Psalm 32:8). "I will guide thee," said the Saviour. He leadeth me. He will be our Guide even unto death," said King David. "He through life has been my Guide," said Fanny Crosby. It is good to be led faithfully. It is bitter agony to be misled, to be led astray.

> All the way my Saviour leads me;
> Cheers each winding path I tread;
> Gives me grace for every trial.
> Feeds me with the living bread;
> Though my weary steps may falter,
> And my soul athirst may be,
> Gushing from the Rock before me,
> Lo! a spring of joy I see;
> Gushing from the Rock before me,
> Lo! a spring of joy I see.

I have experienced winding paths in the African bush. I too have known thirst. What a blessing a drink of pure water is when one's weary steps begin to falter. Your paths may be rough and weary. You too can know the refreshing spring, the living water. Jesus said, "If any man thirst, let him come unto me and drink." (John 7:37). Jesus also said, "Blessed is he that hungers and thirsts after righteousness, for he shall be filled." (Matthew 5:6). Spiritual hunger and spiritual thirst, like physical hunger and thirst, are common to all. The Saviour's invitation to come and drink is for all. It is for you:

> All the way my Saviour leads me;
> O the fullness of His love!
> Perfect rest to me is promised
> In my Father's house above;
> When my spirit, clothed immortal,
> Wings its flight to realms of day,
> This my song through endless ages

Jesus led me all the way;
This my song through endless ages—
Jesus led me all the way.

We have had the testimony of a King of Israel.
We have heard the testimony of a blind hymn
writer. Now hear the testimony of a great leader,
who as an infant was adopted by a princess. He
was brought up in the courts of Pharaoh and edu-
cated to take his place with the Pharaohs. He
rejected his chance to rule Egypt, and took his
place with the despised people of God. Moses sang:
"As an eagle stirreth up her nest, fluttereth over
her young, spreadeth abroad her wings, taketh
them, beareth them on her wings: So the Lord
alone did lead him, and there was no strange
god with him." (Deut. 32:11-12). Moses was old
and ready to die. He had seen years of frustration
trying to lead a rebellious people. He is instruct-
ing his successor, Joshua. Let us listen as the
beloved leader instructs the younger man. "Be
strong and of a good courage, fear not, nor be
afraid of them: for the Lord thy God, He it is
that doth go with thee; He will not fail thee, nor
forsake thee . . . And the Lord, He it is that doth
go before thee, He will not fail thee, neither forsake thee: fear not, neither be dismayed." (Deut.
31:6-8). "He leadeth me," said King David. "He
through life hath been my Guide," said Fanny
Crosby. "He will not fail thee, neither forsake
thee," said Moses. "Lo, I am with you always,
even unto the end of the world," said Jesus. You
can trust His word. He will not fail you.

We Praise Thee, O God

Ancient Israel was exhorted to praise the Lord. King David lists those who should praise the Lord thus: "Kings of the earth, and all people; princes and all judges of the earth: Both young men, and maidens; old men and children; Let them praise the name of the Lord: for his name alone is excellent; his glory is above the earth and heaven." (Ps. 148:11-13).

Praise is part of the Christian's way of life. It is part of every prayer. Praise is a part of our worship. How fitting then that one of our best-loved hymns is a song of praise, as were many of the Psalms.

> We praise Thee, O God! for the Son of Thy love,
> For Jesus who died, and is now gone above.
> Hallelujah! Thine the glory, Hallelujah! Amen.
> Hallelujah! Thine the glory, Revive us again.

This hymn glorifies Jesus, and this truly is the highest type of praise. In the fifth chapter of Revelation we have these beautiful words: "Worthy is the Lamb that was slain to receive power, and wisdom, and riches, and strength, and honour, and glory, and blessing. And every creature which is in heaven, and on the earth, and under the earth, and such as are in the sea, and all that are in them, heard I saying, Blessing and honour, and glory, and power be unto Him that sitteth upon the throne, and unto the Lamb for ever and ever." (Rev. 5:12-13). Truly he has redeemed us to God by His blood out of every nation and tongue and people. That takes in all people everywhere, that is the whosoever.

This hymn was written by a Scottish physician, Dr. W. P. Mackay. After his conversion, Dr. Mackay became a minister of the Gospel and an evangelist. Many people found Christ through his ministry. His conversion, like that of every sinner, was a miracle of grace. His experience is so inspiring that I present it here in the Doctor's own words:

"Before entering publicly my profession as a physician, I was engaged as an assistant in a hospital. In such a place one gets acquainted with a great deal of human suffering. But amidst these things the precious fruit, produced alone by Christian faith, is also to be seen.

"This was nothing new to me, for in the earliest days of my youth I had the opportunity to see such fruit, and especially in the life of my dear mother. She had been a godly, pious woman, quite often telling me of the Saviour, and many times I had been a witness to her wrestling in prayer for my soul's salvation.

"But nothing had made a deep impression on me. The older I grew the more wicked I became. For the God of my mother I did not care in the least, but rather sought by all means to drive Him out of my thoughts. I was in danger of becoming a thorough infidel, but for the voice of my conscience ever accusing and reproaching me. About this time an incident that crossed my life gave it an entirely different course. One day a seriously injured hod-carrier, who had fallen a considerable distance while climbing a ladder, was brought into the hospital. The case was hopeless; all we could do was ease the pains of the unfortunate man. He seemed to realize his condition, for he was fully conscious, and asked me how long he would last. As it was in vain to keep the truth from him, I gave him my opinion in as cautious a manner as I could. 'So long yet! I thought it would be sooner, but He knows best,' he said.

" 'Yes, I believe I know it,' I answered. And the man looked at me endeavouring to smile. 'I understand you very well, but I meant Someone else,' he answered with difficulty. 'Have you any relatives whom we could notify?' I continued. The patient shook his head. He was alone in the world. His only wish was to see his landlady, because he owed her a small sum, and also wished to bid her farewell. He also requested that his landlady send him 'The Book.' 'What book?' I questioned. 'O just ask her for the book, she will know,' was his reply.

"After a week of much suffering he died. I went to see him on my regular visits at least once a day. What struck me most was the quiet, almost happy expression which was constantly on his face. I knew he was a Christian, but about such matters I cared not to talk with him or hear.

"After the man had died some things about the deceased's affairs were to be attended to in my presence.

"What shall we do with this?" asked the nurse, while holding up a book in her hand. 'What kind of book is it?' I asked.

" 'The Bible of the poor man. His landlady brought it on her second visit. As long as he was able to read it he did so; and when he was unable to do so any more, he kept it under his bed cover.'

"I took the Bible and—could I trust my eyes?

It was my own Bible! The Bible which my mother had given me when I left my parents' home, and which later, when short of money, I sold for a small amount. Yes, I had sold it. My name was still in it, written in my mother's hand. Beneath my name was the verse she had selected for me. I stood as if in a dream, but I regained my self-control, managing to conceal before those present my deep emotion. In seemingly indifferent manner and tone I answered the nurse, 'The book is old and has hardly any value, let me keep it, and I will see about the rest.'

"I took the Bible to my room. It had been used frequently. Many leaves were loose, others were torn; the cover was also damaged. Almost every page gave evidence that it had been read very often. Many places were underscored, and while looking through it I read some of the precious verses, and a word I had heard in the days of my youth came back to memory. With a deep sense of shame I looked upon the Book, the precious Book. It had given comfort and refreshing to the unfortunate man in his last hours. It has been a guide to him into eternal life, so that he had been enabled to die in peace and happiness. And this Book, the last gift of my mother, I had actually sold for a ridiculous price.

"I need not add much more. Be it sufficient to say that the regained possession of my Bible was the cause of my conversion.

"The voice of my conscience could no longer be silenced. I found no rest until I arose and came to Him whose hand of love I had so often repulsed, but Who ever thought of me in pity and compassion. By God's mercy and grace I was enabled to believe that 'Christ Jesus came into the world to save sinners,' of whom I seemed to be 'Chief.' "

In the light of Dr. Mackay's testimony, we can feel that this hymn is an expression of his gratitude and thanksgiving to God, for His unspeakable gift.

> We praise Thee, O God! for Thy Spirit of Light,
> Who has shown us our Saviour, and scattered our night.

> All glory and praise to the Lamb that was slain,
> Who has borne all our sins and has cleansed every stain.

> All glory and praise to the God of all grace,
> Who has bought us, and sought us, and guided our ways.

How could he ever regard the Bible lightly again? Or be unconcerned when the voice of God spoke so clearly to his own heart: From the time of Dr. Mackay's conversion the Bible became a new book. For the first time in his experience, it became the Word of God. If the President of the United States got in touch with you by long distance telephone, would you not be deeply impressed? You would drop all else to take that call, and you would cherish every word. Think who called me! The President of the United States! Think of him calling me, little me! But you have a personal message, a royal invitation from the King of Kings to visit Him, and be His guest: It is written in God's own Word, and it is golden, more precious than a mine of gold: "Come unto me, all ye that labor and are heavy laden, and I will give you rest. Take my yoke upon you, and learn of me; for I am meek and lowly in heart: and ye shall find rest unto your souls. For my yoke is easy, and my burden is light." (Matt: 11:28-30). This is a personal message, a personal invitation to you, and it is precious. Think Who it is, Who sends the message! He is the King of Kings, the Saviour of the world, the God of all the universe, the Eternal Father!

You, too, can have the precious experience that Dr. William P. Mackay had, if you will just accept that invitation now. Just open the door of your heart, and let Jesus in, and he will abide with you. When you have received Him into your heart, then you too will praise Him, "Who has borne all your sins, and has cleansed every stain." With all your heart you will sing:

> Hallelujah! Thine the glory,
> Hallelujah! Amen.
> Hallelujah! Thine the glory,
> Revive us again.

Take My Life

Some people want their own way. It is common to see children at play demanding their right to be leader. When we see men and women demanding the same thing we may well wonder what is wrong. I have heard parents say they will break their child's will. A horse with a broken spirit is useless. A man or woman with no will power is a menace to society. They are the pill pushers, the narcotics and drug and drink addicts. These poor people are a constant threat to themselves and to society.

God does not want to break your will. He wants you to give your will to Him. Suppose you *are*

stubborn and selfish and willful? People may say
it is because you are a hard-headed German, a
Dutchman, a Russian, or it's John Bull showing
up. Or is it that you have red or ginger hair?
Perhaps you are a hot-headed Oriental, or a Latin
American. Let's face it. Tell it true and like it
is. That evil temper, your stubborn will, is sin.
A clergyman I know blames his stubbornness on
his mother's side of the family. He need not do
that. Put the blame where it belongs. Are you
too stubborn to forgive and forget? Are you too
proud to say, "I'm sorry."? Has your wounded
pride taken a lot of battering?

If God does not want to break your will, then
what does He want? What can you do with it?
God wants you to give your will to Him. Just
give Him your will, your mind, your heart, your
all. Don't expect it back. Your stubborn will has
caused you enough trouble already, has it not?
You give your will to God. His Holy Spirit sancti-
fies your will. Then it is no longer your own will,
but His will. His will is Holiness. It is your key
to life's richest treasures. It is His will to give
you all things. He has promised, "If ye abide
in me, and my words abide in you, ye may ask
what you will and it shall be done." (John 15:7).
You cannot say you will abide in Him all but
your will. That you will reserve. Yours must be
an entire consecration. It must be a complete
giving up of self to Him to be cleansed by His
Holy Spirit. Sin cannot abide in you while you
abide in Him. Self (the carnal nature) is an enemy
of God. Give your selfish nature to Him.

Take my will, and make it Thine;
It shall be no longer mine;

Take my heart—it is Thine own,
It shall be Thy royal throne.

Francis Ridley Havergal, who wrote this consecration hymn, was in poor health much of her
life. Her father was a clergyman of the Church
of England in Worcester for many years. Miss
Havergal lived in Worcester, London, and Swan-
sea, South Wales for much of her life, apart from
a few trips to Germany and Switzerland. She knew
how frustrating ill health can be. In London on
one occasion, when she was undergoing a severe
personal trial, the Lord gave her this lovely hymn
and she wrote a book on the hymn: *Kept for the
Master's Use.* The book is a gem and I shall
quote from Miss Havergal's own writings:

Keep my will, O Keep it Thine;
For it is no longer mine.

"Perhaps there is no point at which expectation
has been so limited by experience as this. We
believe God is able to do for us just so much
as He has already done, and no more. We take
it for granted a line must be drawn somewhere;
so we choose to draw it where experience ends,
and where faith would have it begin. Even if we
have trusted and proved Him as to proving our
members and minds, faith fails when we would
go deeper, and say, 'Keep my will.' And yet the
only reason we have to give is that it is altogether
His, but that self will crop up again and again.
The result of this, as of every other faithless con-
clusion, is either discouragement and depression,
or, still worse, acquiescence in an unyielded will,
as something that cannot be helped.

"Let us now turn our thoughts to God's
thoughts. Verily, they are not ours. He says He

is able to do exceeding abundantly above all we
ask or think. Apply this here. We ask Him to take
our wills and make them His. Does He or does
He not mean what he says. If He means what
He says, should we not trust Him to do this thing
that we have asked and longed for? Not less
but more. Is anything too hard for the Lord?
Hath he said, and will He not do it? We give
Him no opportunity of proving His great faithfulness to this promise, because we will not fulfill
the condition of reception, believing it. But we
readily believe all that we hear of the unsatis-
factory experience of others.

"It may be that we have not sufficiently realized
all the sin of the only alternative. Our will belongs to self or to God. It may seem a rather
small or excusable sin in man's sight to be self-
willed. But in what a category of iniquity God
puts it!" (II Peter 2:10). Certainly we are without
excuse when we have such a promise to go upon
as "It is God that worketh in you both to will
and to do of His good pleasure."

> Take my life, and let it be,
> Consecrated, Lord, to Thee;
> Take my hands, and let them move
> At the impulse of Thy love.

Is it consistent to ask the Lord to take your life
and let it be consecrated to Him, then expect
to exclude Him when it comes to your will, or
having your own selfish way? I quote again from
Miss Havergal, as she has stated the proposition
with such logic and wisdom.

"Only in proportion as our will is surrendered,
are we able to discern the splendour of God's
will. Conversely, in proportion as we see this splendor of His will, we shall more readily or more

fully surrender our own. Not until we have presented our bodies a living sacrifice can we prove
what is that good and perfect and acceptable will
of God. But in proving it, this continual presenta-
tion will be more and more seen to be our reason-
able service, and become more and more a joy-
ful sacrifice of praise."

> Take my silver and my gold;
> Not a mite will I withhold.
> Take my intellect and use
> Every power as Thou shalt choose.

This matter of one's silver and one's gold
strikes rather close to home. Here is where
self and selfishness get mixed up in one's spiritual
condition. A friend of mine was both surprised
and pleased when I told him his son had given
me a sum of money for our African missions.
He said, "If it has touched his pocketbook, that
is good." Some people have an unapproachable
barrier between their religion and financial pos-
sessions. They act on the assumption that the Lord
is either stingy or miserly as they are, or that
the Lord does not keep His word. Jesus said, "Give,
and it shall be given unto you, good measure,
pressed down, shaken together and running over.
For in the same measure you give, withal, it
shall be given unto you." Try giving it to Him
and see if He does not open the windows of heaven
and pour you out such a blessing that you shall
not be able to receive it. A man once told me
he could not afford to tithe. I told him he could
not afford to withhold his tithe. That tenth is not
yours, but God's. After I had preached a sermon
on tithing in Seattle on one occasion, a man came
to me and said he would not withhold his tithe
from God, as that would be stealing.

Christians would not think of stealing from others, yet they will take what belongs to God and think nothing of it. In the book of Malachi the question is asked: "Will a man rob God? Yet ye have robbed me time without number. Ye ask, wherein have we robbed thee? In tithes and offerings. Bring ye all the tithes into the storehouse, and prove me now herewith, saith the Lord of Hosts, and see if I will not open the windows of heaven and pour you out a blessing, you will not be able to receive it." Will you take what belongs to God and then lose what belongs to you? Will you demand your own way and lose the joy of knowing His perfect will and having delightful fellowship with Him?

> Take my love; My Lord, I pour
> At thy feet its treasure store.
> Take my self, and I will be
> Ever, only, all for Thee.

Give the Lord your will, your love, your life, your self, your all, and find the joy and peace that passes all understanding.

Sowing for the Master

The Bible says, "Blessed are they that sow beside all waters." and "They that sow in tears shall reap in joy. He that goeth forth and weepeth, bearing precious seed, shall doubtless come again with rejoicing, bringing his sheaves with him." (Ps. 126:5-6). Sowing seed is often hard work. Many times I have watched the farmers in the Midlands of England sowing their crops while a flock of sea gulls followed them hungrily seeking the precious grain just planted by the hard-working farmer.

It is often that way with those who sow the spiritual seed. There will be those who scoff and ridicule your work and testimony. They will say you are wasting your time. You should be spending your time and money at some more profitable work. I think of two very good friends of mine who spend many dollars every year for scripture portions to give out. The Rev. Ray Johnson, veteran missionary, who just returned from Africa, is a splendid example. He was our business manager in Monrovia, Liberia, until recently when he returned to the States. Ray gave out about 40,000 little Bibles while he was in Africa this last term, which lasted about two years. I remember hearing one man hold Ray up to ridicule and suggest he could spend his time in a more dignified way. I presume he thought that giving out tracts and speaking to the man and woman or boy and girl in the street about the Saviour is just not quite the thing. Brother Johnson is known by many, many Africans as Uncle Ray and he is loved and respected by most. I am sure when the sheaves are brought in there will be many credited to Rev. Ray Johnson, missionary.

Another minister friend of mine goes into the prisons and hospitals and trailer courts seeking the lost. Wherever he goes, in prison, hospital or on the street, the Rev. Douglas Noble has his pockets full of tracts and scripture portions to give to those he meets. There are many men and women in many parts of the United States and Canada who found Christ through Brother Noble or a Bible portion he gave them.

He saved my life. I went into a men's clothing

store in North London. The proprietor greeted me with enthusiasm when he learned I was from the Pillar of Fire Society at Hendon. "Where is that other chap that visited me last year?" he asked. I told him that he had returned to the United States. He said, "He saved my life." I asked him to tell me about it and here is his story.

He said he was thoroughly discouraged and beaten. He had planned to end his life. He was going to commit suicide. That day the Rev. Norman Sillett walked into his place of business. "He spoke so kindly to me, I just knew he was a man of God, and I decided against suicide. He told me how to pray. When he left I did pray and the Lord forgave me. I am a Christian now." My friend Norman Sillett gives out thousands of Gospel magazines and books. Only eternity will reveal just how many others found the Saviour because he called on them.

> Sowing in the morning, sowing seeds of kind-
>   ness,
> Sowing in the noontide, and the dewy eve.
> Waiting for the harvest and the time of reap-
>   ing,
> We shall come rejoicing, bringing in the
>   sheaves.

The Rev. Knowles Shaw, author of the above hymn, was born in Butler County, Ohio, October 13, 1834. His father died when Knowles was a young lad. Before he died Albin Shaw told his son to "be good to your mother and prepare to meet your God." This advice was accompanied with the family violin as a present for Knowles. It could be the violin had been given to the boy some months before his father's death, as Knowles was already showing some aptitude for music.

Such advice is often forgotten or ignored by young people, but young Knowles Shaw took it seriously. He worked hard to help support his mother. The story of his conversion is indeed unusual. Knowles attended a big party and played his violin while the young people had a great time. While all were rejoicing at the party, Knowles realized that he had neglected his promise to his dying father. He prayed for forgiveness there and then. In church the following Sunday he made his confession and gave his testimony. Later he began to testify in meetings and finally got up courage to preach his first sermon.

In January 1855 Knowles married Martha Finley. She laboured with him sowing the precious seed until death parted them many years later. Mr. Shaw became an evangelist and singer. He was six feet four inches tall and must have looked like the George Beverly Shea of his day. Sometimes he illustrated his sermons with his own poetry. To illustrate a sermon he preached, taking his text from the Prophet Daniel, he wrote the poem:

At the feast of Belshazzar and a thousand of
　　his lords,
While they drank from golden vessels as the
　　Book of Truth records—
In the night as they revelled in the royal
　　palace hall,
They were seized with consternation—'twas
　　a hand upon the wall!

Chorus:

'Tis the hand of God on the wall!
'Tis the hand of God on the wall!
Shall the record be, "Found wanting!"

Or shall it be "Found trusting!"
While the hand is writing on the wall?

That Gospel song is almost forgotten today. But in Sunday schools and churches all over the country and in many other lands you will hear the children and adults alike singing "Bringing in the Sheaves."

Sowing in the sunshine, sowing in the shadows,
Fearing neither clouds nor winter's chilling
  breeze;
By and by the harvest and the labour ended,
We shall come rejoicing, bringing in the sheaves.

Going forth with weeping, sowing for the
  Master,
Though the loss sustained our spirit often
  grieves;
When our weeping's over, He will bid us
  welcome,
We shall come rejoicing, bringing in the
  sheaves.

In Knowles Shaw's years of faithful sowing he received more than eleven thousand people into the church and saw them converted. His death was a sad one and one cannot help thinking of that other double tragedy when Phillip Bliss, author of "Hold the Fort" and "I Am So Glad That Jesus Loves Me," was killed with his wife in a train accident in Ohio. Knowles Shaw had concluded a five-week evangelistic campaign in Dallas, Texas. He boarded the train to return to his home and loved ones in Columbus, Mississippi. The train left the track and twenty-seven passengers were injured. The evangelist was caught by wreckage and died before he could be rescued. His last words were: "Oh, it is a grand thing to rally people to the Cross of Christ." He had spent his years doing just that and who knows how many will stand before the throne of God one day washed in the blood of the Lamb, and will point to Knowles Shaw and say, "He brought me to the Saviour."

Nearer, Still Nearer

Troubles, problems, trials, sorrow—all come to most people at some time in their lives. The way people react to those troubles, trials and sorrows depends to some extent upon the resources on which they have to draw. In the hour of severe trial, happy is that person whose God is the Lord. He is our help and strength, a very present help in time of trouble. He said, "Call upon me in the day of trouble and I will deliver thee" (Ps. 50:15). So if you are troubled or perplexed and do not know which way to turn, this message may be for you.

King David tells us he had reached the bottom. He almost despaired, then he called on the Lord, and He delivered him (Ps. 116:1-2). Without going into detail he tells us in the 40th Psalm, "He brought me up also out of an horrible pit, out of the miry clay, and set my feet upon a rock, and established my going." Isaiah tells us that the Lord "loved him out of the pit" and then cast all his sins behind his back (Isa. 38:17). With the same thought in mind of deliverance to the distraught and needy, we read the words of the Lord in Jeremiah 31, "Yea, I have loved thee with an everlasting love, therefore with lovingkindness have I drawn thee." (Jer. 31:3).

A mother in great sorrow asked me if God cared. Her little child had sickened and died. I assured her that God does care. He loves you with an everlasting love. He loves you so much that He is unwilling to leave you alone one moment. He has said, "I will not fail thee, I will not leave thee nor forsake thee." If you feel all alone in your trials, draw near to Him and He will draw near to you. He is only far away when we stray from Him.

> Nearer, still nearer, close to Thy heart,
> Draw me, my Saviour, so precious Thou art;
> Fold me, oh fold me, close to Thy breast,
> Shelter me safe in that "Haven of Rest,"
> Shelter me safe in that "Haven of Rest."

You need the shelter and protection that is found only in Him, the Rock of Ages. Sometimes you are frightened even of your fears. How could anyone else understand? The psychiatrist would blame frustrations and tap you for your money, while the fire burned and the trouble remained. When the Saviour draws you close to Himself, the very love of Jesus dissolves and cleanses and removes those troubles and sorrows.

> Nearer, still nearer, nothing I bring,
> Nought as an offering to Jesus my King;
> Only my sinful, now contrite heart,
> Grant me the cleansing Thy blood doth impart,
> Grant me the cleansing Thy blood doth impart.

The writer of these beautiful words, "Nearer, still Nearer," was Mrs. C. H. Morris (Lelia N. Morris). As a young girl, she felt the need of a personal Saviour. She felt far away and did not know how to draw near to God. She tells us her own story. She went forward three different times seeking the Saviour and forgiveness for her sins. Nothing. Then an elderly man came out and "laid his hand on my head, and said 'Why, little girl, God is here and ready to forgive your sins.'" She accepted His forgiveness and opened her heart to Him. She was sheltered safe in that "Haven of Rest." She

was not free from troubles, but she was no longer
tossed by the waves of the sea of sin and doubt.
She was "in Christ Jesus. Amen."

> Nearer, still nearer, Lord, to be Thine,
> Sin, with its follies, I gladly resign;
> All of its pleasures, pomp and its pride,
> Give me but Jesus, my Lord crucified,
> Give me but Jesus, my Lord crucified.

Pride seems to keep a lot of people away from
Christ and His fulness. "What will my friends think
of me? Will I have any friends if I seek Christ?"
The devil appeals to your selfish ambitions and
your pride. He does not care how much you suffer
because of your "sinful heart." The Lord wants
to forgive those sins and give you rest.

Mrs. Morris wrote many other hymns, including
the children's hymn, "The Fight Is On." Another
that is a favorite of mature Christians is "Sweeter
as the Years Go By." One of her invitation hymns
had a most unusual beginning. Mrs. Morris had
attended services at Mountain Lake Park. George
Sanville tells the story. A visiting minister, Rev.
L. H. Baker, brought the message. The song leader
was the hymn writer, Dr. H. L. Gilmore. After
the message a lady of some refinement went forward. Mrs. Morris saw that the lady was having
some personal struggle. She knelt by her and with
her hand on her shoulder said, "Just now your
doubtings give o'er." Dr. Gilmore leaned over and
added, "Just now reject Him no more." The Rev.
Baker, who was listening, came forward and added,
"Just now throw open the door." To which Mrs.
Morris simply added, "Let Jesus come into your
heart." Those words without alteration became
the chorus of her new hymn, "Let Jesus Come into
Your Heart."

If you are tired of the load of your sin,
Let Jesus come into your heart;
If you desire a new life to begin,
Let Jesus come into your heart.

Mrs. Morris said of herself, "I am just a channel,
I just open my mind and let the story flow through."
She wrote over 1200 hymns and poems, of which
many are in regular use. Just now open your heart
and mind. Let Jesus come into your heart.

Nearer, still nearer, while life shall last,
Till safe in Glory my anchor is cast;
Nearer, my Saviour, still nearer to Thee,
Nearer, my Saviour, still nearer to Thee.

Jesus, I My Cross Have Taken

The cross is not popular today. It never has
been coveted except as a symbol. People will wear
it around their necks, they will display it on a coat
lapel or dress. But who wants to be carried on
one? Who wishes to be nailed to a cross? Jesus
said, "If any man will come after me, let him deny
himself, and take up his cross, and follow me."
(Matt. 16:24). St. Paul, a Jew, a Pharisee, a Roman,
and a man of learning and education said, "I am
crucified with Christ, nevertheless I live, yet not
I but Christ liveth in me; and the life that I now
live in the flesh, I live by the faith of the Son of
God, who loved me, and gave himself for me."
(Gal. 2:20). He gloried in the cross. To him the
cross meant death to sin, and life with Christ. From
his Roman prison, St. Paul could write, "For me
to live is Christ." (Phil. 1:21). That is the life more
abundant.

Many young people are leaving home today. To

some young people, the life of the hippie, the nar-
cotic or the society rebel is "groovy." I visited
one of these young people in prison recently. In
prison he gets a free "pad"—free room and board
—but no heroin. If he does not do as he is told
he is put into solitary confinement. That is where
he was when I visited him. He complained of the
cold, and of the lack of hot water in prison. He
thought his parents did not understand him. Con-
trast his position and that of many young society
people with that of Mary Bosanquet.

Was It Fair? Mary Bosanquet was the daughter
of a wealthy merchant in England. She belonged
to "society." She wore the finest and most expensive clothing and jewelry. Her father knew all the
"right" people. Whatever Mary wanted she only
needed to buy. What more could she want? But
something like a bombshell fell in that Bosanquet
home.

Mary was invited to attend meetings held by
the Methodist Society. Without telling her father,
she went to a service, then more services.

Then It Happened! Wealthy Mary Bosanquet
was converted. She felt as though she were floating
on clouds. Oh, the joy of it! She told her father.
He was ashamed. His own daughter, who belonged
to society, was dropping out to join the Society
of Methodists! How cruel, how ungratful. What is
more, Mary invited her brothers to the meetings
and spoke to them about their souls. She began
to dress plainly like the Society of Methodists. That
added insult to injury, and her father came to her
with a demand. "Mary, there is a promise that
I require you to make. That is, that you will never,
now or hereafter, try to make your brothers what
you call 'Christian.' " Mary replied, "Father, I

dare not consent to that." "Then, if you refuse to consent to that you force me to put you out of my house." Mary replied, "According to your view of things I do." Her father chided, "You don't appreciate what I provide for you. You wear the plain clothes of 'those people.' "

How could she explain that she loved her father very much and appreciated his interest and provision? "If I but think on the word holiness, or of the adorable name of Jesus, my heart seems to take fire in an instant, and my desires are more fixed on God than ever before. As I cannot go with you any more to places of amusement, so neither can I wear the expensive clothes you buy me any more. I must be God's and His alone."

Her father told her to pack her things. He called the family coach and soon Mary, with her belongings in one trunk, entered the coach to leave home; to follow Christ. Mary told her father of a promise God had given her. "Father, God has promised me that I shall 'walk with Him in white.' " Her father allowed her young maid and companion, who was also a Christian, to accompany her. Imagine a young man or woman being "turned on" by the thought of holiness or the name of Jesus!

From the homes of the rich, with the gabled and terraced houses, the servant's quarters, lush and beautiful gardens, the coach travelled to the homes of the poor in Laytonstone. Mary's new home had two rooms and a dismal view of chimney stacks and filthy yards of her neighbors. She had not brought candles. She borrowed a table and two chairs. She had this peace that passeth understanding.

Jesus, I my cross have taken,
All to leave and follow Thee;

Destitute, despised, forsaken,
Thou from hence my all shalt be;
Perish every fond ambition,
All I've sought and hoped, and known;
Yet how rich is my condition,
God, and heaven are still my own!

She was driven to her knees many times, and there she found Him, Jesus, the fairest of ten thousand. The Lord reminded her: "When thy father and thy mother forsake thee, then the Lord shall take thee up." He did not fail her. The Lord kept His promise. Mary said, "Why, I am brought out of the world, and I have nothing to do but to be holy—holy in body and spirit. What a happy soul I am! Truly my abode is a bit of heaven." God provided a friend and helper for Mary; her name was Sarah Ryan. They moved to Hoxton in Islington. Their abode was with the poorest of the poor. They had prayer meetings in their home and one woman after another asked to join them. Their numbers grew to such proportions that Mary appealed to John Wesley to send them a preacher for Sunday services, which he did.

One Thursday evening Mary was speaking to a large crowd in her own kitchen when four rough-looking men with clubs tramped in. Mary went on with the service although a neighbor came in and whispered to her that the men were bringing a mob to stone them. At the close of the meeting Mary handed out leaflets which she had prepared, telling the rules of the Society. She handed a copy to each of these ruffians. They accepted them and left without any disturbance.

Let the world despise and leave me,
They have left my Saviour too;
Human hearts and looks deceive me;
Thou art not like man, untrue;

And while thou shalt smile upon me,
God of wisdom, love, and might,
Foes may hate, and friends may shun me;
Show Thy face, and all is bright.

It was in the year 1760 that Mary's father put
her out of their home. Just 37 years later, Henry
F. Lyte was born in Scotland. (See my book,
Next Hymn Story, Please!). While Lyte was preparing for the ministry in Ireland, Mary was
ministering to the poor and outcasts of Laytonstone and Hoxton. Young Lyte, later Vicar of
Lower Brixham, heard Mary's story. He was so
inspired by her courage and purity of life that he
wrote this lovely hymn.

Mary took a number of children into her home
and about thirty adults. They depended wholly
on the Lord for support. God, who is a Father
of the fatherless, never failed to supply their needs.

Man may trouble and distress me,
'Twill but drive me to Thy breast;
Life with trials hard may press me,
Heaven will bring me sweeter rest.
O 'tis not in grief to harm me,
While Thy love is left to me,
O 'twere not in joy to charm me,
Were that joy unmixed with Thee

Men did trouble her as they often did the Society
of Methodists. They broke her windows often and
threatened her with many injuries. Yet God pro-
tected her and never was she physically harmed.
Mary was offered a farm in Yorkshire, where
she would be able to provide more easily for her
growing family of orphans, now thirty-five in
number.

Saintly John Fletcher of Madeley. Mary had
more than one proposal of marriage. However,
when the saintly John Fletcher, Vicar of Madeley,

asked her to marry him, she finally accepted.
It was John Fletcher whom John Wesley chose
as his successor to take over the Methodist Society leadership. Mr. Wesley spoke of Mr. Fletcher
as the most saintly man he had ever known. "One
equal to Mr. Fletcher I have not known, no, not
in a life of fourscore years."

God has a plan for everything. Soon after Mary
accepted Mr. Fletcher's offer of marriage a man
came offering to buy her farm. Mary was able
to provide homes for all the children and to give
each child and adult, dependent upon her, an
annual income of fifty-five pounds.

Two people better suited for the work of their
Master could hardly be found. Yet in four short
years the saintly John Fletcher, who was to have
led Methodism after the death of John Wesley,
took ill and died suddenly before the aged Wesley.
Mary continued working in Madeley for thirty
years after the death of her beloved husband.
As she approached the end of her long and happy
life, Mary Fletcher said, "It is the Lord who
blesses me. He lifts His hands and shows that
I am graven there."

> Haste thee on from grace to glory,
> Armed with faith and winged by prayer;
> Heaven's eternal days before thee,
> God's own hand shall guide thee there.
> Soon shall close thy earthly mission,
> Swift shall pass thy pilgrim days,
> Hope shall change to glad fruition,
> Faith to sight, and prayer to praise.

"He lifts His hands and shows that I am graven
there," said Mary Bosanquet Fletcher. "Lo, I
have graven thee on the palms of my hands,"
we read in Isaiah. Jesus said, "I will not forget

thee." "Remember me," said the dying thief.
"Today thou shalt be with me," said Jesus. You
can trust Him.

More About Jesus

What would life be without Jesus? Without
Jesus there would be no hospitals, there would
be no orphanages for children, and the homes
for the aged and mentally infirm would not exist.
In this connection I have put down a few thoughts.
A beautiful cathedral without Jesus is only cold
stone and mortar. A tent or a cottage in the
African bush with Jesus is a hallowed place. A
throng of people without Jesus is a crowd. Two
or three people with Jesus make a church. Life
without Jesus is rough and sinful. Life with Jesus
is joy and peace.

Miss Eliza E. Hewitt, author of some of our
beautiful hymns, was told the sad news of a
mother's aching heart. Her son had just passed
away. To comfort the mother she sent these
lines:

Christmas with Jesus

Christmas in the Father's house,
His first Christmas there;
All the many mansions shining
In the light most fair.
All the golden harp strings ringing,
All the angel voices singing,
That bright anthem once again,
Which they sang o'er Bethlehem's plain.

Miss Hewitt was the author of that beautiful
hymn, More About Jesus. Some of her other
hymns are just as well known: When We All Get

to Heaven; Give Me Thine Heart; Sunshine in
My Soul; and Will There Be Any Stars in My
Crown?

> More about Jesus would I know
> More of His grace to others show;
> More of His saving fullness see,
> More of His love who died for me.

Eliza E. Hewitt was born in Philadelphia,
Pennsylvania, June 28, 1851. Her father, James
S. Hewitt, and her mother Zeruiah, were godly
parents. They read the Bible in their home and
had frequent hymn fests. All the family could
sing many hymns from memory.

Miss Hewitt started on a career as a public
school teacher. A serious accident resulting in
a spinal injury caused her to give up her career
as a teacher in public schools. However, she continued to teach in Sunday school whenever her
painful malady permitted. While she was confined
to her home because of the excessive pain, in
1887, she leafed through her Bible studying and
feasting on the promises of God. At this time she
wrote a prayer that bares the secret desire of
her heart. It is "More About Jesus." The words
are simple and full of meaning. It is indeed a
perfect Christmas prayer. It is an ideal prayer
to start the new year, and a fitting petition for
beginning another day.

> More about Jesus let me learn,
> More of His holy will discern;
> Spirit of God, my Teacher be,
> Showing the things of Christ to me.

On one occasion Jesus said to His disciples,
"Without me ye can do nothing." (John 15:5).
It is well for us to remind ourselves that if Jesus
is not the center of our lives, we are self-centered.

It is hardly necessary to say that a selfish life is one misspent. It is indeed fitting when the sinner sees Jesus in your life. The little English missionary to China, Gladys Aylward, toiled for years in the mountain villages of North China. Apart from an occasional mule driver or mountain farmer who found Christ through her faithful teaching, it seemed she was not reaching far. True, she had bought or adopted a few children, and some young women had accepted Christ through her guidance. Her life was truly a prayer, More About Jesus. Perhaps her finest hour in that mountain village was the day the Mandarin gave a dinner in her honor. He spoke of her work and her God. He told how she had stopped a prison riot, how she had tended the sick and wounded and dying after a Japanese raid on their town. Then turning to Miss Aylward he said, "I would like to embrace your religion, I want to become a Christian." When the ungodly person turns to you and says, "I want Jesus, too. I will become a Christian," that is the greatest joy one can know. It is even greater than the joy one finds in those first moments of his own new-found peace in Christ, if such is possible.

> More about Jesus; in His word,
> Holding communion with my Lord;
> Hearing His voice in every line,
> Making each faithful saying mine.

We are told in the Revelation that His voice is like the sound of many waters. Anyone who has had the joy of sitting by a rushing mountain stream will know the meaning of this description of the voice of Jesus. To hear His voice is indeed joy and peace. David Livingstone told of his experience at the Zambezi. A hostile chief told him

he would die if he tried to cross that river. With
this thought in mind the great missionary doctor
sought solace in his Bible. He read the words
of Jesus, "Lo, I am with you alway, even unto
the end of the world." He wrote in his diary,
"That is the word of a Gentleman, and that is
the end of it. Should such an one as I flee? I
shall take soundings this night for longitude and
latitude and cross over in the morning in day-
light." The Lord was true to His promise and
Dr. Livingstone was not molested.

> More about Jesus on His throne,
> Riches in glory all His own;
> More of His kingdom's sure increase,
> More of His coming, Prince of Peace.

Jesus said, "My peace I give unto you." You
can experience this peace, the gift of God's love
at not only Christmas time, but every day of your
life. In the words of another of Miss Hewitt's
hymns you can say, "There is sunshine in my soul
today, more glorious and bright, than glows in
any earthly sky, for Jesus is my Light. You can
know the joy of those Judaean shepherds when
they heard the angel saying to them, "Unto you
is born this day . . . a Saviour, which is Christ
the Lord." When you give Him your heart you
will be able to sing with that heavenly chorus,
"Glory to God in the highest, and on earth, peace,
goodwill to men."

> More, more about Jesus
> More, more about Jesus.
> More of His saving fullness see,
> More of His love who died for me.

Turn Your Eyes Upon Jesus

Out here in California we are often told to get involved, or don't get involved, depending on the issue or cause. Without hesitation I can advise you to "get involved." Get involved in the greatest cause in all the world today. It is far ahead of "ban the bomb" or "leave Viet Nam now" or "war on poverty." It is the greatest. Get involved in lifting burdens, in saving souls. Young people today are frightened and troubled. They worry about the future. Jesus said, "Don't worry. Don't be troubled." "Let not your heart be troubled, neither let it be afraid." (John 14:27). Jesus spoke those words of advice and comfort to His followers and believers and not to the scoffing, godless world. They do have plenty to fear, and no cause for hope. There are always those who worry. Nearly every family has one or two. On one occasion before my wife and I set sail for Great Britain on the UNITED STATES, friends told us of the great storms at sea. The morning the ship was to sail a friend called to say that he had heard there was a strike on ship and that the ship would not sail. This strike rumor proved false. We had faith in the ship, in its captain, and what is more important, in God. We had a delightful voyage. Some passengers said they had never known it so calm in winter.

A great seaman and fisherman was standing on board his ship with his fellow seamen. There was a gale blowing and it was a rough sea. Although it was dark these two seamen saw something that frightened them. The elder of the two

was so horrified he cried out in fear. A familiar
voice spoke reassuringly, and said, "It is I, be
not afraid." (Matt. 14:27). The old seaman answered, "Lord, if it be thou, bid me come to
thee on the water." Jesus told him to come. Had
any seaman or fisherman or anyone else ever
tried this before? Peter was actually walking on
that boisterous and troubled sea. Some well-
meaning friend on the ship may have called out,
"Peter, look out. You'll never make it. Just look
at those waves, and look at that sea!" Peter did
look at the waves, and he began to sink. But
when he was sinking his only thought was of the
Saviour, and he cried out, "Lord, save me." Immediately Jesus reached out His hand and saved
him.

No doubt Peter had reason to remember this
experience years later, on more than one occasion. It was not long after this experience that
Peter, who had been the frightened old seadog,
became as fearless as a lion. Truly, the Lion of
the Tribe of Judah (Jesus) was with him and
in his heart. He who had recently been cowered
by a young girl, who faced him with his connection with Jesus of Galilee, and caused him
to deny his Lord and Saviour, was completely
transformed. What a transformation!

> O soul, are you weary and troubled?
> No light in the darkness you see?
> There's light for a look at the Saviour,
> And Life more abundant and free!

Peter, who had been troubled and frightened
into denying his Lord by a young girl, was truly
in darkness. On the day of Pentecost the Light
of the World was shining through his heart and
life and flooding his soul with all His radiant

beauty. Now he was bold as a lion. Facing an angry mob he told them truly they were traitors and murderers. He told them plainly and without fear that they were guilty of crucifying their Saviour, their Messiah. Those unbelieving ones were caught in a trap and cried for mercy and deliverance from all their sins. Peter had told them, "Therefore, let all the house of Israel know assuredly, that God hath made that same Jesus, whom ye crucified, both Lord and Christ." When they heard that, they were pierced to the heart, and cried out, "Men and brethren, what shall we do?" Peter, too, had been in a similar condition once. When sinking he cried to Jesus for help, and the hand of his Saviour lifted him up. Peter told the crowd to repent of their sins and look to Jesus. His blood would cleanse them from all their sins.

> Thro' death into life everlasting
> He passed, and we follow Him there;
> Over us sin no more hath dominion—
> For more than conquerors we are!

Now, if you go to Jesus, as He has invited you to do (Matt. 11:28), and begin to serve Him, you will find plenty of worriers. There will be those to give you poor advice. They mean well but they are not following the risen Saviour themselves. The devil will create great billowy waves so difficult, so high, that at times you will feel you are sinking. The devil will get you to look at the storms of life and your fears, if possible, instead of looking to Jesus. No sea of trouble can boil and crash loud enough to drown the voice of the Son of God, who said, "Be of good cheer. It is I. Be not afraid."

Turn your eyes upon Jesus,
Look full in His wonderful face;
And the things of earth will grow strangely
    dim
In the light of His glory and grace.

This chapter is affectionately dedicated to my
daughter, Pamela Aldstadt, and her friend, Corry
Slikker Young, who sang the chorus of "Turn
Your Eyes Upon Jesus" every Sunday, at the end
of our morning worship service, for over two years.

No One Ever Cared for Me Like Jesus

A broken heart is sometimes the result of sin
and a misspent life. Many a mother has died of
a broken heart because of the sins of a wayward
son, daughter, or husband. The hymnwriter,
Charles Weigle, knew what is meant by a broken
heart. God sustained him through the sorrow of
his wife's leaving him, and enriched him with
all the comfort of His undying love. Five years
later he was able to write the beautiful hymn,
"No One Ever Cared for Me Like Jesus."

Charles Weigle was born at LaFayette, Indiana, November 20, 1871. His parents were immi-
grants from Germany. His father and uncle owned
a bakery and grocery store in LaFayette. Mrs.
Weigle prayed that her son Charles would follow
God's way for his life and her prayers began to
be answered when Charles was converted before
his twelfth birthday. While he was studying for
a musical career at Cincinnati Conservatory of
Music he felt God was calling him to be a preacher
of the Gospel. He was a Methodist, but preached

for the Friends in Pasadena, California, and years later joined the Baptists. One of his first hymns was, "I am Glad I Came Home."

> I would love to tell you what I think of Jesus,
> Since I found in Him a Friend so strong and
>   true;
> I would tell you how He changed my life com-
>   pletely,
> He did something that no other Friend could
>   do.

Not long after his marriage, Rev. Weigle began to travel as an evangelist. After their daughter was born, Mrs. Weigle began to show resentment at being the wife of an evangelist and being left at home so much. One evening when he came home his wife told him she was leaving. She said his way was not for her. She wanted the glamour way, the broad way. That very night she took her little daughter and left home. She went to Los Angeles to seek thrills. A short time later she lay dying and asked her daughter to try to "find your father and ask him to pray for me." She died before her husband knew of her illness. Those bright lights could not bring the thrill of sins forgiven and the dying woman sought the prayers of her saintly husband. Truly, God alone can change the life completely. He is a Friend so strong and true.

Five years after her death Charles Weigle remarried. This time he found more harmony and spiritual unity in his marriage. His wife was one with him in his ministry and loved the Lord with all her heart.

One day Weigle was sitting at the piano in his home and as his fingers ran over the keys the thought came to him, "No One Ever Cared

for Me Like Jesus." He began to meditate on
God's love and care for him. In a short time he
had composed the tune and words of a hymn that
can best be described as a thumbnail biography
of its author.

> All my life was full of sin when Jesus found
> me,
> All my heart was full of misery and woe;
> Jesus placed His strong and loving arms
> around me,
> And He led me in the way I ought to go.

This indeed is the condition of every born-again
Christian. Because of sin the heart of every sinner
is filled with misery and woe. Sin has its pleasures
which last for a season. The drunkard forgets
his sorrows and troubles for a brief moment while
he is acting like a feeble-minded wreck under
the influence of drink. When he sobers up his
sins and misery come back to taunt him a hundred
times over. Jesus alone can take sin from your
life and mine. You need His strong and loving
arms around you to lead you in the way you
ought to go.

> Every day He comes to me with new assur-
> ance,
> More and more I understand His words of
> love;
> But I'll never know just why He came to
> save me,
> Till some day I see His blessed face above.

The Bible says the "path of the just is as
the shining light that shineth more and more until
the perfect day." Surely it is true that every day
with Jesus is sweeter than the day before. If you
would understand God's Words of love you can
do so more and more as you read it and cherish

it in your heart. King David said, "Oh, how I love Thy law. It is my meditation day and night." Yet we can never know all of God's love. Why He came to save sinners will always be a delightful mystery until we see His lovely face. And oh the joy when I shall see Him face to face, and have Him throw His loving arms around me and say, "Well done, enter thou into the joy of thy Lord." Just to hear Him speak your name will through the ages be glory for you.

> No one ever cared for me like Jesus,
> There's no other Friend so kind as He;
> No one else could take the sin and darkness
>   from me;
> Oh how much He cared for me.

In the Epistle of Peter we read: "Casting all your care upon Him for He careth for you." How true this is. He cares for you. You have misery and woe, sorrow and trouble. Other people are often unsympathetic or they do not understand. How could they understand. You are you and no one really understands you like Jesus. Because He understands you so well He is kind and loving. He alone can take the sin and darkness from your life. He alone can forgive sin and set you free from your chains of misery and woe. He said, "They that seek me early shall find me." Seek Him and find for yourself that there is no other Friend so kind as He.

Ashamed of Jesus

The Christian is the most privileged individual of all. He is bought with a tremendous price, even the blood of our sinless Saviour, Jesus Christ.

He is exalted to the position of Son of God. The King of Kings has chosen the heart of His blood-washed as His throne.

A missionary doctor friend of mine, who spent over forty years in China, told me this story. An elderly Chinese merchant was led into the hospital by a small lad. The merchant was blind. The doctor operated to remove cataracts and the man could see. What a marvellous experience! He was eternally grateful. He took the doctor's hand and said, "Doctor, I will be your servant as long as I live. My whole being both thanks and praises you."

The Christian who has been saved from death owes his life, his all to Him who loved him and gave Himself for him.

Some Christians say, in effect, "I know I am a Christian, but I could never witness to anyone. Oh, I could never give out a Gospel or a tract to anyone. What would people think? They might think I had gone daft on religion."

Now why should the born-again Christian be ashamed to speak of his Saviour? When you are ashamed to witness, is it your own shortcoming or weakness of which you are ashamed? Remember you are not asked to exalt self, but Christ. He says, "Ye are my witnesses."

St. Paul, a Jew, an intellectual of his day, took up the cross and became forever dead to the world and self. He said, "I am crucified with Christ." How strange for a self-respecting Jew. But St. Paul was no longer concerned about what people would think of Paul. He was dead. Dead men are not easily offended. How can you offend a dead man? He was dead, nevertheless he said, "I live, yet not I, but Christ liveth in me, and

the life that I now live in the flesh, I live by
the faith of the Son of God, who loved me, and
gave Himself for me." (Gal. 2:20). Could St. Paul
ever be ashamed of Him who saved him from
the lowest pit? Never!

You say you could never witness to the lost
sinner, and tell him of his only hope of life and
peace? Of whom are you ashamed? St. Paul
said, "For I am not ashamed of the Gospel of
Jesus Christ, for it is the power of God unto salvation, to everyone that believeth; to the Jew
first and also to the Greek (Gentile)." (Rom.
1:17). Of whom are you ashamed?

Ashamed of Jesus! That dear Friend? I ob-
served when attending a political convention that
there were delegates present from every state
in the United States and from Puerto Rico and
the Virgin Islands. How proudly they displayed
their colors! They wanted everyone to know who
they were, and from whence they came. When
the name of President Eisenhower was presented
as their candidate for another term of office, the
roar of acclamation was deafening.

The Scriptures tell us that when Jesus, our
Saviour, comes back to earth, the announcement
of His name will cause every man, woman, and
child to bow their knee and proclaim Him as Lord
of Lords and King of Kings (Phil. 2:10-11). That
will be the greatest mass demonstration the world
has ever known. What a glorious day that will
be! We shall see our Saviour face to face. However, during that time there will be some who
are unprepared for His coming. They will cry
out for the rocks and the mountains to fall on
them and hide them from the face of Him who
sitteth upon the throne (Rev. 6:16).

Jesus, and shall it ever be,
A mortal man ashamed of Thee?
Ashamed of Thee, whom angels praise,
Whose glory shines through endless days?

Yes, incredible as it may seem, the majority of so-called Christians are ashamed of Jesus. They do not choose to do or say anything that would brand them as His followers. They dress like the world. They talk and act like the world. It no longer shocks people to hear profanity, men and women frequently taking the Lord's name in vain. Recently when I spoke to a businessman for taking the Lord's name in vain, he told me he was a church member, a church worker. Sin has become fashionable.

One may smoke, drink, gamble, and take the Saviour's name in vain; in moderation, of course. Is it true that these people are Christians? Can a Christian curse His God, His Saviour, His Only Hope?

Ashamed of Jesus! that dear Friend
On whom my hopes of heaven depend!
No; when I blush, be this my shame,
That I no more revere His name.

This impressive hymn was written by Joseph Grigg, in London, when he was but ten years of age. He wrote it after he heard a sermon on Mark 8:38, "Whosoever therefore shall be ashamed of me, and my words, in this adulterous and sinful generation, of him shall the Son of Man be ashamed, when he cometh in the glory of his Father, with the holy angels." Later young Joseph became a minister and preached in Silver Street, London, for many years. His hymn, "Behold a Stranger at the Door," was written after he was ordained.

People will cheer their favorite player at Lord's Cricket Grounds, the Oval, or Yankee Stadium, but nominal Christians are ashamed of their dearest Friend—the only One who can save them from everlasting contempt, eternal banishment from light, the Light.

Jesus is your only Hope. He has promised you an hundredfold in this life and eternal life in the world to come. He does not make promises today and forget them tomorrow. He has promised to be with you in trouble (Psalms 91:15 and Matthew 28:20). He has promised to receive you, whoever you are, wherever you are, and whenever you come to Him (John 6:37). Will you go to Him now? He will never turn you away.

O Could I Speak the Matchless Worth

A young man was dying on a British navy ship off the West African coast. He had been wounded in a running sea battle. His leg had been all but severed from his body. The young lad, just eighteen years old at the time, felt that his end had indeed come. He began to pray desperately. He prayed that God would have mercy and forgive his horrible sins. He prayed much of the day and night, and the next morning the doctor seemed surprised to find him still alive and his leg definitely better. The surgeon told him his leg could be spared. God had answered his prayer for forgiveness and had touched his body. How wonderful! How marvellous!

O could I speak the matchless worth,
O could I sound the glories forth,
Which in my Saviour shine,
I'd soar and touch the heavenly strings,
And vie with Gabriel while he sings,
In notes almost divine,
In notes almost divine.

Indeed his leg was saved, his life was spared! Samuel Medley studied for the ministry after his release from the Royal Navy and lived to preach the everlasting Gospel for almost forty years.

The Rev. Samuel Medley was born at Cheshunt, Hertfordshire, England, June 23, 1738. Charles Wesley had been converted almost a month before Samuel's birth, on that memorable Whit Sunday, May 21, 1738. Charles' brother, John, was born again three days later on Wednesday, the 24th. (See *Next Hymn Story, Please!* by Wilbur Konkel.) Samuel's parents had been pious, God-fearing Christians, but like so many other young men and women brought up in Christian homes, he went astray. Perhaps it was his life in the Royal Navy that turned him; or could it have been a desire to kick over the traces, like the Prodigal Son? Who can say why young men and young women who have been brought up in Christian homes go astray? We are sure that Satan wants to sift them like wheat, but thank God for the prayers of Christian parents and friends that follow them right into the pen where they are feeding swine. So God answered prayer for Samuel Medley and He answered prayer for John and Charles Wesley; He answered prayer for me and He will answer prayer for you. To God be the glory!

I'd sing the precious blood He spilt,
My ransom from the dreadful guilt

Of sin and wrath divine;
I'd sing His glorious righteousness
In which all perfect heavenly dress
My soul shall ever shine.
My soul shall ever shine.

Rev. Samuel Medley was ordained a minister of the Baptist Church in 1766 and took up his first ministerial post the same year at Watford. It is believed he wrote the above hymn, "O Could I Speak the Matchless Worth" during his first year at Watford, England. One hundred years after the fire of London, one hundred years after John Bunyan had begun to write *Pilgrim's Progress* in Bedford jail, another Pilgrim had started a fire that was to blaze for many years, and indeed is still blazing in the hearts of all who love to sing "His glorious righteousness."

Every true born-again Christian, like John and Charles Wesley, John Bunyan and Samuel Medley, loves to sing of his Redeemer. He never grows weary of telling of God's great love to sinners and power to save to the uttermost all who will repent and turn to Him. God's Word says that "righteousness exalteth a nation" and God's righteousness exalts His saints, the bloodwashed.

I'd sing the characters He bears
And all the forms of love He wears,
Exalted on His throne;
In loftiest songs of sweetest praise
I would to everlasting days,
Make all His glories known,
Make all His glories known.

We love to sing of our Redeemer and we never do tire of telling how He rescued us from the "dreadful guilt" of sin and wrath divine. Jeremiah loved to tell how his Ethiopian friend, Ebedmelech, rescued him from that horrible dungeon, and saved his life. Just so he loved to tell how God had whispered His love to him saying, "I have loved thee with an everlasting love: therefore with lovingkindness have I drawn thee." (Jer. 31:3). Just so Samuel Medley vowed that to "everlasting days" he would make all His glories known.

From Watford, Mr. Medley went to Liverpool, where his triumphant ministry of 27 years in that city was interrupted by his triumphant death. How lovely is the last verse of this hymn. You, too, may know the joys of sins forgiven and have the delight of making His glories known, if you will do like Samuel Medley did at the age of 18, and turn to God with all your heart and pray in simple faith and trust, "God, be merciful to me, a sinner."

> Well, that delightful day will come
> When my dear Lord will call me home,
> And I shall see His face;
> Then with my Saviour, Brother, Friend,
> A blest eternity I'll spend,
> Triumphant in His grace,
> Triumphant in His grace.

The Light of the World Is Jesus

Matthew tells us in his Gospel of the birth of Jesus, and of the wise men who sought and worshipped Him. It is a wise man who will seek Jesus, and when he has found Him, worships Him. St. Luke tells us of the birth of Jesus also and adds the delightful account of the heavenly choir singing, "Glory to God in the highest, and on earth peace, good will toward men." (Luke 2:14). I believe those words and accompanying music are recorded in heaven. What a thrill if we may have

the joy of hearing that song again one day! John
begins his Gospel with the account of the coming
of Jesus as the Light. "This is that Light that light-
eth every man that cometh into the world." (John
1:8). Jesus said, "I am the light of the world."

So, with the coming of Jesus, the Saviour, to
Bethlehem, the Light of the World came to dispel
the darkness from men's hearts. Jesus said He did
not come into the world to condemn the world, but
to save the world. Strange as it may seem, men
did not want to be saved. Instead they began to
condemn the Saviour and to reject the Light. "This
is the condemnation, that Light is come into the
world, and men loved darkness rather than light,
because their deeds were evil." (John 3:19).

During the twenty-four years I spent in Great
Britain, I always enjoyed the display of lights at
Christmas time. During the war years we were
blacked out. In winter the days are short. By three
in the afternoon the sun begins to set and darkness,
gloom and rain cover the earth. That is Great
Britain. How delightful then to see the lights and
to hear the carollers singing of the Saviour's birth.
The lights of Oxford Street, and Regents Street,
of Princess Street in Edinburgh are a joy to behold.
Those lights are a refreshing reminder of Jesus,
the Light of the World.

My first Christmas in Africa was something
else. It was the dry season. Being near the equator
the sun was burning hot. For days there had been
almost twelve hours of unbroken sunshine. I was
at Tournata, the R. G. LeTourneau town on the
edge of a jungle of beauty and mystery. In villages
round about, the huts were lighted with kerosene
lamps. There Christmas has not become big business. Jesus is Christmas and Christ is all. At ten

minutes past six on the 25th of December the sun
burst forth in all its splendor to dispel the darkness
in those jungle villages, and to proclaim to the
world that "the Light of the World is Jesus." That
was a good day. Except that I was separated from
my family, I have never had a more delightful
Christmas Day. I brought the message at eleven
that day, and the Light of the World shone into
my heart with all His splendor.

> The whole world was lost in the darkness of
>   sin;
> The Light of the world is Jesus;
> Like sunshine at noonday His glory shone in,
> The Light of the world is Jesus.

When God created the heavens and the earth,
darkness was upon the face of the deep. Then God
commanded the light to shine out of the darkness;
and there was Light. The story of that Light is
the story of Jesus. "For God, who commanded the
light to shine out of darkness, hath shined in our
hearts, to give the light of the knowledge of the
glory of God in the face of Jesus Christ." (II Cor.
4:6). There was a plague of darkness in Egypt,
but in the homes of the Israelites there was light.
When Jesus was born in Bethlehem, conditions were
much the same. The people were in darkness.
Darkness that could be felt. It was gloom that pene-
trated the hearts of men and women everywhere.
Darkness, gloom, misery and sin; the whole world
was lost in the darkness of sin. Then Jesus came.
The Light of the world is Jesus. Like sunshine at
noonday His glory shone in. The Light of the world
is Jesus!

> No darkness have we who in Jesus abide,
> The Light of the world is Jesus;
> We walk in the Light when we follow our Guide,
> The Light of the world is Jesus.

What does light do for the world? It gives life.
Without the light of the sun there could be no life
on the earth. The sun gives warmth. What can live
without light and warmth? What does Jesus mean
to the world? He is the Light and the Life. I am
not a scientist. I do not know about the many light
rays. But I know that the Sun of Righteousness
has arisen in my heart with healing in His wings.
He dispelled the darkness of sin and, like sunshine
at noonday, His glory shone in.

> Ye dwellers in darkness with sin blinded
>   eyes,
> The Light of the world is Jesus;
> Go wash at His bidding, and light will arise,
> The Light of the world is Jesus.

Fish have been found in the Mammoth Cave
that are blind. Living in that darkness, so far un-
derground, they have lost the use of their eyes.
There are many people who have lived in sin and
darkness so long that they know nothing else. They
know only darkness and gloom. Unlike the fish in
a dark cave, man was meant for the light. He
thrives in light. Man was made by God, to enjoy
Him. When the Light of the World comes into a
heart to dispel darkness of sin, that person is born
from above. He is a new person. Old things have
passed away and, behold, all things become new!

> No need of the sunlight in heaven, we're told,
> The light of the world is Jesus;
> The Lamb is the light in the City of Gold,
> The light of the world is Jesus.

This lovely hymn was written by Phillipp Bliss.
He had no second name, so he took the last "p"
from Phillipp and signed his name P. P. Bliss. He
was born in a log cabin in Pennsylvania and never
heard a piano until he was ten years old. As a

barefoot boy he had gone to town to sell berries from door to door. Hearing the music of a piano in one home the lad was thrilled. He entered the house without knocking and tiptoed over to the piano. When the lady who was playing saw him, she ordered him out of the house. Today his hymns are played and sung around the world. His children's hymn, "I am so glad that our Father in Heaven," or "Jesus Loves Even Me," is loved by old and young alike. I confess that it is one of my favorites. He also wrote "Dare To Be a Daniel," and "Only an Armor Bearer."

About a year after he wrote "The Light of the World Is Jesus," Phillipp Bliss and his wife and their two children went to visit his mother in Buffalo, New York. It was to be Christmas with mother and back in Chicago by the New Year. After Christmas they left their two children with their grandmother and boarded a train to return to Chicago. That train left the rails on a bridge at Ashtabula, Ohio, and was enveloped in flames. A survivor stated that he saw Mr. Bliss fighting his was back into a flaming car to rescue his wife. They both lost their lives.

By strange coincidence their trunk had been placed on another train and arrived safely in Chicago. Friends opened the trunk and found a hymn that Bliss had just completed, his last. It was quite fittingly entitled, "I Will Sing of My Redeemer." This hymn was set to music by Mr. Bliss's friend, James McGranahan.

Like P. P. Bliss you too can know the joys of sins forgiven. You, too, can then say:

> Sweetly the Light has dawned upon me
> Once I was blind, but now I can see.
> The Light of the world is Jesus.

I Need a Great Saviour

Have you ever felt the power of sin in your life? If you know what it is to be tempted beyond endurance, then you know the need of a Great Saviour. What can you do? Where can you go? The Lord said, "Look unto me, and be ye saved, all the ends of the earth. For I am God and there is none else." (Isa. 45:22). Again we read, "Neither is there salvation in any other, for there is none other name under heaven given among men, whereby we must be saved." (Acts 4:12). When you are tempted and tried, then you need someone who can help you. Jesus can help you, Jesus alone.

> I must tell Jesus all of my trials;
> I cannot bear these burdens alone;
> In my distress He kindly will help me;
> He ever loves and cares for His own.

This beautiful hymn, "I Must Tell Jesus," was inspired by the almost desperate cry of a poor woman in sorrow and trouble. The pastor, Elisha A. Hoffman, ministering at that time at Lebanon, Pennsylvania, spent part of his time calling on the poor and destitute people who live on the other side of the tracks. This lady had much sorrow, and it seemed she had more than her share of troubles. She poured out her sorrow into the sympathetic ears of her visiting pastor. In desperation she wrung her arms and cried, "What shall I do? Oh, what shall I do?" Reverend Hoffman replied, "You cannot do better than to take all your sorrows to Jesus. You must tell Jesus." As he was leaving the lady's face lighted up as she said, "Yes, that's it, I must tell Jesus." The pastor then quoted several comforting and helpful passages of scripture, "Come unto me, all ye that labour and are heavy-laden and I will give you rest." (Matt. 11:28). "If we confess our sins, He is faithful and just to forgive us our sins, and to cleanse us from all unrighteousness." (I John 1:7). "Cast thy burden upon the Lord, and He will sustain thee." These scriptures, along with the injunction to tell Jesus, encouraged the poor distraught soul to cry to God for forgiveness and mercy. She was converted.

Reverend Hoffman went home from this scene rejoicing in God, His Saviour. He said later, "Do you wonder that with these words ringing in my ears, I made my way home and God gave me the inspiration to write this hymn?" Elisha A. Hoffman was born in Orwigsburg, Pennsylvania, May 7, 1839. His father was a minister and young Elisha was converted at an early age. In 1866 he received a license to preach, and in the same year he was married. In 1869 the Hoffmans were invited to go to Cleveland, Ohio, and help in editing a denominational publication known as *The Living Epistle.* Some of Mr. Hoffman's first hymns appeared in this publication. In 1876 the Hoffmans published a booklet entitled "Happy Songs for the Sunday School." This booklet contained a hymn by Hoffman which is still sung in many parts of the world, "Glory to His Name." Not long after this successful publication, Mrs. Hoffman passed away at the age of thirty-two. It was a few years after the death of his wife that Reverend Hoffman returned to Pennsylvania, this time to Lebanon, where he wrote "I Must Tell Jesus."

I must tell Jesus all of my troubles;
He is a kind, compassionate Friend;
If I but ask Him, He will deliver,
Make of my troubles quickly an end.

How true these words. Many, many troubled
souls have pillowed their heads on this comforting
thought. The policeman tells the criminal, who was
caught in the very act, "Tell it to the judge." In
fear, the unhappy misfit often conceals the facts
or deliberately lies, hoping for clemency or mercy
from the judge. Often the judge, who has his own
troubles to solve, gets through the case as quickly
as possible. At times he shows leniency; sometimes he is severe. Often the judge is unable to
cope with the problems of society's outcasts who
shuffle back and forth through those halls of justice. The judge has no time to hear your personal
problems. There are many other cases awaiting
his attention. You must move on. But there is One
to whom you can tell all your troubles. He is your
Friend. He is the only One who can always forgive
and have mercy. He can deliver you. Set you free.
Sometimes the judge must sentence the accused.
Prison bars seem so cold and unsympathetic to
your cries. But Jesus can make of your troubles
quickly an end.

But then, how does this apply to you? You have
never been a criminal. You have never stood at
the bar of justice. You hever had the judge say
to you, "Six months and five hundred dollars fine."
You and I are nice people. We are respectable.
Wait! Someone is saying, "All have sinned and
come short of the glory of God." You have just
been apprehended by the Judge of all the earth.
He said, "Unless you repent, you shall all likewise

perish." Yes, that means you. There are no exceptions. But there is good news for you. You are condemned. You are lost. But the Son of Man came to seek and to save that which was lost. If I but ask Him, He will deliver, make of my troubles quickly an end.

> Tempted and tried, I need a great Saviour,
> One who can help my burdens to bear;
> I must tell Jesus, I must tell Jesus;
> He all my cares and sorrows will share.

When I was in London, I met a man from Scotland. He had a tool-sharpening and key-making business. On one occasion I visited him at his request and he poured out his heart to me. He was in trouble at home. His wife was threatening to leave him because of his drinking. His son was beginning to follow his father's footsteps to the bars. As he poured out his heart, he asked, "What can I do?" "Should I try Alcoholics Anonymous?" I said, "You need a person. A Saviour. The fellowship of others is good, but you need forgiveness and pardon. Reform is not for you. It is not a patched-up job you want. You need to become a new man. You need Jesus. You must be born again. You must become a new creation."

"But how is this possible?"

"You must tell Jesus, the One who can bear your burdens; make of your troubles quickly an end." True, there will always be problems, but there will always be a Saviour, your Friend, to hear and to forgive.

Scotty told me a story that would make good seed for another Sherlock Holmes detective novel. However, Scotty's story is true. Some weeks after we had prayer together in his shop, two men called on Scotty and asked him if he wanted to make

some money. He replied that that was why he
was in business. They said what he was doing
was peanuts. They could offer him five thousand
pounds for fifteen minutes work. All he had to
do, so these men told him, was to make a duplicate
of two keys from a nearby bank. They could bring
him the keys at noon when all the other employees
were at lunch. He could work fast and they would
return the original keys to the bank before the
others knew what had taken place. Would Scotty
like that kind of money?

"What did you tell them?" I asked. "I told
them to get packing and never come back," was
Scotty's reply. "But I want to tell you one thing.
If it had not been for God's help I would have
been in my cups when they came around, and
I could not have resisted them. I thank God He
has helped me not to touch a drop since you prayed
with me that day." What a great Saviour! Hallelujah! You may not be tempted in the same way
as my Scottish craftsman friend was, but you,
too, need a great Saviour. Jesus can help you,
Jesus alone.

Oh how the world to evil allures me!
Oh how my heart is tempted to sin!
I must tell Jesus, and He will help me
Over the world a victory to win.

Jesus said, "If you ask anything in my name,
I will do it." He is able to do exceedingly abundantly above all we ask or think. He can deliver
you from the world and its evil allurements. You
cannot bear your burdens alone. You cannot bear
those evil temptations alone. You must tell Jesus,
Jesus can help you.

You must tell Jesus! I must tell Jesus!
I cannot bear my burdens alone,

I must tell Jesus! I must tell Jesus!
Jesus can help me, Jesus alone.

If you will ask Him, He will deliver, make of
your troubles quickly an end.

I Heard the Bells
on Christmas Day

Have you ever been tempted to ask, "Where
is God?" Or, "Does God care about me?" In
some moment of utter despair have you ever
asked, "Is God dead?" These doubts have come
to many people, because we are so much of the
earth, earthy. We fumble, we stumble, and we
fall. Then somewhere in the darkness a light shines
through. You hear his voice saying: He leadeth
me beside the still waters, He restoreth my soul.
Surely goodness and mercy shall follow me all
the days of my life. You hear Him again: "Fear
thou not, for I am with thee, be not dismayed,
for I am thy God. I will strengthen thee, yea,
I will help thee; yea, I will uphold thee with the
right hand of my righteousness." (Isa. 41:10).

Henry Wadsworth Longfellow tells of some
doubts he had in a moment of despair. Those
were times to rend and try man's soul. War was
raging between the States. There were troubled
times in Europe and in many lands. The Italian
states were starting their struggle for a united
Italy. Austria was in open conflict with Italy.
Brothers were fighting over the question of slavery
in America. Christmas came with its message
sung by the angels of peace on earth, good will
to men. "Unto you is born this day in the city

of David, a Saviour, which is Christ the Lord."
The bells were ringing out the glad news of peace
on earth, good will to men. Let us listen to Longfellow's experience again as he adds his voice
to the beautiful song of the angel chorus.

> I heard the bells on Christmas Day
> Their old familiar carols play,
> And wild and sweet the words repeat,
> Of peace on earth, good will to men.
>
> I thought how, as the day had come,
> The belfries of all Christendom
> Had rolled along the unbroken song
> Of peace on earth, good will to men.
>
> And in despair I bowed my head;
> "There is no peace on earth," I said.
> "For hate is strong and mocks the song
> Of peace on earth, good will to men."
>
> Then pealed the bells more loud and deep;
> "GOD IS NOT DEAD: NOR DOTH HE
>   SLEEP;
> The wrong shall fail, the right prevail,
> With peace on earth, good will to men."
>
> Till ringing, singing on its way,
> The world revolved from night to day,
> A voice, a chime, a chant sublime,
> Of peace on earth, good will to men!

Again, we too bow our heads and repeat the words,
"There is no peace on earth, for hate is strong
and mocks the song of peace on earth, good will
to men." War rages in Viet Nam. A world for whom
Christ died is destroying itself. Famine stalks and
slays the millions of India and China.

A shadow hangs over the City of Peace, Jerusalem. The peace of death now stalks through the Holy Land. Many people in Bethlehem, Jerusalem, and the rest of the Holy Land will bow their heads and mourn their dead; as all Christendom sings again the old familiar strains of peace on earth, good will to men.

Just over a year ago I stood in old Jerusalem and saw the crowds milling along the Via Doloroso. A man and woman staggered under the burden of a cross as they labored to carry it up the steps. They were re-enacting, reliving the stages of the cross. I stood in the Garden of Gethsemane. Beneath the olive trees I, too, bowed my head. The strains of "Not my will, Thine be done" brought tears to my eyes as Arlene Lawrence, at my request, sang, " 'Neath the Old Olive Trees."

I overlooked the hill of Calvary and heard my Lord saying, "Father forgive them, for they know not what they do." As the agony of my sins weighed Him down, He bowed His head and cried: "My God, my God, why hast Thou forsaken me?" Then, in triumph, His shout of victory rang out as He cried, "It is finished!" He was wounded for my transgressions. He was bruised for my iniquities, the chastisement of my peace was upon Him; and with His stripes I am healed. I entered the Garden Tomb. The caretaker, Mr. Solomon J. Mattar, told in simple but inspired words the sweet story of Jesus again. He told how He triumphed over sin, death, and the grave. Death is swallowed up in victory. Our Lord is not dead, He is risen, He lives! Yes, He lives within my heart.

We went to Bethlehem and rejoiced and joined with the angels as they sang the sweetest story ever told, of peace on earth, good will to men. My heart leaps up as that Star of Bethlehem

shines in all His splendor. Unto you, unto me,
is born this day in the City of David, a Saviour,
which is Christ the Lord. Is it true? Was He
wounded for my transgressions? Was He bruised
for my iniquities? Yes, it is true, wonder of
wonders, and with His stripes I am healed! He
brought me up also out of an horrible pit, out
of the miry clay, and set my feet upon a Rock,
and established my goings. And he hath put a new
song in my mouth, even praise unto our God (Ps.
40:2-3).

With King David, I invite you to come, and
I will declare unto you what He hath done for
my soul. He brought me up also out of an horrible
pit, where my sins dragged me down. With Longfellow I joyfully declare, "God is not dead, nor
doth He sleep." He lives! He lives! Christ Jesus
lives today! You ask me how I know He lives?
He lives within my heart." Hallelujah, what a
Saviour! I rebelled against Him. My sins nailed
Him to the cross. In bitterness and shame I cried:
"Have mercy on me, oh Lord. Forgive my transgressions." I forgot Him, I strayed and wandered
away. But He sought me, and found me. In lovingkindness Jesus came. In love He lifted me. I
thought I was alone, but He said, "Lo, I have
loved thee with an everlasting love. Therefore,
with lovingkindness have I drawn thee." (Jer.
31:3). "Lo, I am with thee alway, even to the
end of the world." "I will never leave thee, nor
forsake thee."

Great Is Thy Faithfulness

One of my favorite portions of scripture for

many years has been Jeremiah's declaration of
faith: "This I recall to my mind, therefore have
I hope. It is the Lord's mercies that we are not
consumed, because His compassions fail not. They
are new every morning: great is Thy faithfulness."
(Lam. 3:21-23).

This scripture became a living reality in my
own experience during those dark war days of
1939 to 1945. Night after night we were bombed,
but every morning God was still there. Never
did He fail us. We committed ourselves into His
loving care morning by morning. Each night as
the enemy planes came over, we cast our care
upon Him. I quoted the scripture to myself. I
used it in my prayers and I always delighted in
preaching on the text, and still do. Therefore have
I hope. Those were dark days. At times they
seemed hopeless. It was in those darkest hours
that God proved His faithfulness to me. We were
so near death. Yet it is the Lord's mercies that
we are not consumed, because His compassions
fail not. They are new every morning: great is
Thy faithfulness!

When Billy Graham came to Harringay in 1954,
I heard the hymn, "Great Is Thy Faithfulness,"
based on this scripture, for the first time. George
Beverly Shea sang the hymn with the great London
Choir. I was thrilled. Our missionary, Miss Harriet
McCormick, obtained the sheet music and we sang
it in our chapel at Hendon. From that time on
it became one of my favorites. How true these
words are!

Great is Thy faithfulness, O God my Father,
There is no shadow of turning with Thee;
Thou changest not; Thy compassions they fail
   not;
As Thou hast been, Thou forever wilt be.

"Every good gift and every perfect gift is from above, and cometh down from the Father of Lights, with whom is no variableness, neither shadow of turning." (James 1:17). God is faithful. He does not fail. His compassions, they fail not. He cares for the lilies, He cares for the sparrows. How can He fail me? How can He forget you? You are of more value than many flowers or birds. He will not, He cannot, forget you. He has graven you on the palms of His hands (Isa. 49:16). He was wounded for your transgressions (Isa. 53:3). Like His great universe, He is always here. After the darkest night, the sun comes up with its rosy splendor and warms and brightens all it reaches. So God is always there in your darkest hour. He does not turn away from you. Not even by a faint shadow. As Thou hast been, Thou forever wilt be. Because He is our Father, and because He suffered so much for us, yes He even died for us, therefore His compassions will never fail. He has loved us with an everlasting love.

> Summer and winter, and springtime and
>   harvest,
> Sun, moon, and stars in their courses above,
> Join with all nature in manifold witness,
> To Thy great faithfulness, mercy, and love.

This beautiful hymn was written by T. O. Chisholm. He was born in a log cabin in Simpson County, Kentucky, July 29, 1866. When young Thomas was 21, he got a job as associate editor of a Kentucky newspaper, in Franklin County. It was a weekly, but it gave the young man an opportunity to write and while he was in this position an evangelist came to that community. God used this evangelist to bring Christ to Thomas Chisholm. From the moment of his conversion,

young Chisholm dedicated his life and all to his
Master, the King of Kings. That evangelist was
Dr. H. C. Morrison. He invited Thomas to be office
editor of the *Pentecostal Herald* in Louisville. In
less than three years his health broke down and
Thomas had to go back to business. For a time
he was an insurance salesman, then he became
a travelling evangelist in the Methodist Church.
Again his health failed and he alternated between
insurance and writing for the rest of his life. Almost thirty years after his conversion, Thomas
Chisholm was living in New Jersey. He sent several
poems to Dr. William M. Runyon, a Methodist
pastor-composer then living also in New Jersey.
With the poems, Chisholm sent a request for Dr.
Runyon to write hymn tunes for his poems. Dr.
Runyon was inspired with the poem, "Great Is
Thy Faithfulness." His musical setting to these
beautiful words made the hymn a favorite. It is
only fair to state that George Beverly Shea and
the choirs of the Billy Graham Crusades around
the world have contributed to the popularity of
this lovely hymn.

>   Great is Thy faithfulness! Great is Thy faith-
>   fulness!
>   Thy own dear Presence to cheer and to guide;
>   Strength for today and bright hope for to-
>   morrow,
>   Blessings all mine, with ten thousand beside!

Jesus said, "My peace I leave with you." Great
peace, the gift of God's love. Things seem to be
falling to pieces around our ears. Riots and mur-
ders and rebellion seem to have become the order
of the day. It has become popular for even members of the clergy to question God's love; His
very existence is denied by many. Yet like the

warmth of the noon-day sun, His presence cheers and guides me.

King David said, "God is our refuge and strength." (Ps. 46). After an extremely hard day and a painful and restless night, have you ever wondered how you would ever get through another day? In that dark moment God is there, and He can be your strength for today. What a precious thought—He is our bright hope for to-morrow. All these blessings are mine, they are yours, and ten thousand beside!

> Great is Thy faithfulness! Great is Thy faith-fulness!
> Morning by morning new mercies I see;
> All I have needed Thy hand hath provided—
> Great is Thy faithfulness, Lord unto me!

Has He not promised, "Lo, I am with you alway, even unto the end of the world"? Amen.

Jewels

A jewel may be of great value or it may be of doubtful worth. A diamond cutter in London once told me that the way a diamond is cut and polished has much to do with its ultimate value. He told how he had ruined a diamond once by a mistake in cutting. He said that the original jewel in the rough may be quite large, but by the time it is submitted to cutting and trimming it becomes small in comparison to its original size. The Kur-I-Nur diamond, which is one of the largest cut diamonds in the world, and one of the most beautiful, is in the Imperial crown of Edward VII of England. I have seen it many times and have taken visiting friends to see it in the Jewel House in the Tower of London. That diamond had to be cut and polished most carefully. Without that cutting and polishing, no one would be able to enjoy its exquisite beauty.

We, too, like jewels, need cutting and polishing to bring out our true beauty. The true beauty of the jewel is under the surface. So the true beauty of a boy or girl is within. Only the Master Jeweler, or Lapidary, can assay the worth and value of a soul, a boy or girl, a man or woman. To Him you are precious, for indeed He purchased you with His own blood (I Peter 1:18-19). In fact, the beauty of an individual shines brightest when Jesus comes into his heart and others see His beauty in him. We have a hymn known and loved by children and adults alike. It is "His Jewels."

> When He cometh, when He cometh
> To make up His jewels;
> All His jewels, precious jewels,
> His loved and His own.

> Like the stars of the morning
> His bright crown adorning,
> They shall shine in their beauty,
> Bright gems for His crown.

This beautiful hymn is based on the scripture, "And they shall be mine, saith the Lord of hosts, in that day when I make up my jewels; and I will spare them, as a man spareth his own son that serveth him." (Mal. 3:17). The Lord Jesus Christ wants to make you one of those bright and precious jewels. The difference between a worthless stone and a precious jewel is Jesus. A man with whom I recently spoke was a case in point. He was dirty and unshaven. His eyes were red and glazed. His hair was uncombed. His steps were slow, his voice coarse and cracked. He was old and worn at 50. I told him of the Saviour, but he ridiculed His

name. My heart went out to him, a soul for whom
Christ died, wallowing in the slime of drink and
sin. He wanted another drink. Jesus wants to give
him living water. He prefers the dregs of sorrow
and sin. He is someone's son, someone's brother.

> He will gather, He will gather
> The gems for His kingdom;
> All the pure ones, all the bright ones,
> His loved and His own.

Some day Jesus is coming back to this sin-
troubled earth. What a day of rejoicing that will
be! I want to see Him, don't you? Just one glimpse
of Him in Glory will make all our trials and problems of this life seem worthwhile. But to have
Jesus present you to God the Father as one of His
jewels will be beyond our powers to express in
words. Think of His taking a vile, unlovely sinner
and washing him in His own blood and beautifying
him with Himself! So that it is no longer I but
the beauty of Jesus one sees in me and in you.
You will be one of the pure ones, spotless and flaw-
less, in that day when He makes up His jewels.
What a day that will be! When the saints of all
ages will shine in all His splendour!

> Little children, little children
> Who love their Redeemer,
> Are the jewels, precious jewels,
> His loved and His own.

How Jesus loves the children! He took them up
in His arms and blessed them. His blessing is still
there. It is because of this that Satan is trying in
every possible way to destroy the child, physically,
spiritually, and mentally. Children are continually
being told that this kind of grog or that kind will
make him shine. That if he wants to truly live he

must drink this or that. He is told how a cigaret
is supposed to taste. That it sets him apart from
the crowd. When the child comes out of his school
he may be met by older children or men or women
offering him a "reefer" or a "joint," or, perhaps,
a pill. That precious child for whom Christ died
is being threatened on every side by a degrading,
sadistic, fiendish enemy.

The Author's Voice. The author of "His Jewels"
was a minister of the Gospel, Reverend William
O. Cushing. He was born in Hingham, Massachu-
setts, December 31, 1823. Sometime after his or-
dination, it is not clear just how long, the Reverend
Cushing realized that he was losing his voice. The
day came when he was no longer able to preach
the Gospel he so much loved to proclaim. His voice
was gone. He could speak only in a whisper. No
one who has not had a similar experience could fully
realize what that meant to a young clergyman.
At this time the Shepherd's Psalm was of much
comfort to him. He knew what it meant to descend
into the valley. His had been the bitterness of dis-
appointment. He was cast down, but not defeated.
He lifted his eyes to the Lord, from whom came
his help and strength. He made a re-dedication to
Christ for time and forever. One of his hymns re-
flects his personal experience and his deliverance.
Once again a child of God was able to prove the
promise, "Call upon me in the day of trouble, and
I will deliver thee, and thou shalt glorify me." (Ps.
50:15). From the depths of affliction he cried and
God comforted him and gave him the words of
this beautiful hymn:

   Down in the valley with my Saviour I would
      go,

Where the flowers are blooming and the
sweet waters flow;
Everywhere He leads me, I would follow on,
Walking in His footsteps till the crown be
won.

Follow, follow, I would follow Jesus,
Anywhere, everywhere, I would follow on;
Follow, follow, I would follow Jesus,
Everywhere He leads me I would follow on.

Down in the valley with my Saviour I would
go,
Where the storms are beating and the dark
waters flow;
With His hand to lead me, I would never,
never fear;
Danger cannot fright me if my Lord is near.

Down in the valley or upon the mountain
steep,
Close beside my Saviour would my soul ever
keep;
He will lead me safely in the paths that He
has trod,
Up to where they gather on the hills of God.

We are promised that if we suffer with Him we
shall reign with Him. With heaven in view, Saint
Paul spoke of being cast down but not forsaken,
troubled, yet not distressed; perplexed, yet not in
despair. Languishing in a Roman prison, his body
aged and tired and sick, he was able to look above
the clouds to see the Bright and the Morning Star—
the Sun of Righteousness, shining in all His kingly
splendor. His body racked with pain from stoning
and scourging and neglect, he faced the end of this
earthly suffering. His testimony: "I have fought
a good fight, I have finished my course, I have
kept the faith; henceforth there is laid up for me
a crown of righteousness, which the Lord, the right-

eous judge, shall give me at that day: and not to
me only, but unto all them also that love His ap-
pearing." (I Tim. 4:7-8).

Saint Paul lived for his Lord and Saviour, Jesus
Christ. What a joy when he entered into the presence of His Saviour to behold Him! What a sight
to see all those shining jewels whom he had found
for Christ when he was trudging over the mountains of Turkey, Syria, and Greece! Some would
be there from Caesar's Palace in Rome, some from
Damascus and Jerusalem. But what of the countless ones who found the Saviour through Paul's
letters!

You cannot be Saint Paul, but you can be one
of our Saviour's jewels. You, too, can have the
Saviour with you. To have Him is better than to
have a mine of gold.

In Times Like These

We are living in the most wonderful time and
period of world history. Man has circled the moon.
Heart transplants have been performed in many
parts of the world. Millions of people all over the
world witnessed the inauguration of a new President of the United States by way of satellite. Yet
1969 seemed to be a year of revolt. Young revolu-
tionaries (hoodlums) on our campuses call our pro-
fessors, law-enforcement officers, the Governor of
California, and even the President of the United
States, pigs. To be sure, these young trouble mak-
ers are a small minority, a handful. However, history tells us that Hitler seized power in Germany
with a few fellow roughnecks. Stalin came to power
in Russia over the dead bodies of millions of White

Russians. It was a handful of key people who seized power in Poland, Hungary, Rumania, East Germany, and Czechoslovakia.

I feel sure that the majority of young people in our colleges and universities want an education. They are eager to get on with their classes and studies. This is no doubt true in Paris, London, Berlin, and Rome as well. A few young people have been able to bring chaos to many fellow students.

The words of Saint Paul spoken just over nineteen hundred years ago seem strangely up to date. "And that, knowing the time, that it is now high time to awake out of sleep; for now is our salvation nearer than when we believed. The night is far spent, the day is at hand; let us therefore put off the works of darkness, and let us put on the armor of light. Let us walk honestly, as in the day . . . But put ye on the Lord Jesus Christ, and make not provision for the flesh, to fulfill the lust thereof." (Rom. 13:11-14).

I believe most young people today want a better life. They want the very best there is in life. Their problem is where to find this life. Jesus said, "I am the way, the truth, and the life, no man cometh unto the Father but by me." (John 14:6). Jesus also said, "I am come that they might have life and have it more abundantly." (John 10:10). He came to give you the very best. It is yours for the asking. I found this thrilling account of a young teenager the other day, and would like to share it with you. I quote the account in full. It is from the Marion, Indiana *Leader-Tribune.*

A Mississinewa High School teacher asked her students to write an essay stating what they would do, or how they would spend their time if they knew this would be the last week of their lives. Just over a week after Billie Kay Bothwell wrote this essay, she met her death in a dreadful car accident with three other young high school students. Her essay:

"Today I live: a week from today I die. If a situation such as this came to me I should probably weep. As soon as I realized there are many things to be done, I would try to regain my composure.

"The first day of my suddenly shortened life I would choose to see all of my loved ones and assure them I loved them all. On the evening of my first day I would, in the solace of my room, ask God to give me strength to bear the rest of my precious days and give me His hand so that I could walk with Him.

"On the second day I would rise to see the rising sun in all its beauty that I had so often cast aside for a few moments of coveted sleep.

"The third day I would spend alone, or not completely alone, but in the woods, in the presence of God's creation and goodness around me. I would see, undoubtedly for the first time, many things I had not seen before.

"On the fourth day I would prepare my will. The small, sentimental things I possess I would leave to my family and friends. This being done I would go on my way. I believe I would go to my mother and spend the day with her. We were always very close together and I would want to reassure her of my love especially.

"On Friday, my life almost ended, I would spend the time with my minister, speaking to him of my spiritual life and seeking advice on how I could improve it in the future. I would like to go with him to visit those who are ill. I could silently be thankful that I know no pain, and yet I know my destiny. On this evening I would be with the special someone in my life and talk of his problems and try to comfort him. More than this, I would be happy and gay in spite of the fact that we would never meet again.

"Saturday I would spend visiting the sick and shut-ins; I had so often put that off to another day. On this, the night before my death, I would probably be awake much of the night, fearing my impending death, and yet preparing for it, knowing that God is by my side.

"Upon awakening Sunday morning I would make all my last preparations, and then taking my Bible, I would go to Church to spend my last hours in prayer to ask God for courage to face the remaining hours, that I might die gracefully, and that my life might have some bearing on someone that would have glorified His Holy Name. Yes, my last hours would not be spent in agony, BUT IN THE PERFECT HARMONY OF JUST MY GOD AND I."

Just over a week after this lovely young girl wrote this essay, she was ushered into eternity in a tragic car accident near her home town in Marion, Indiana. How refreshing to read of a young teenager who would desire the fellowship of Christ, the outdoors, His creatures, and creation and her parents and family as a last wish. There was no mention of drink, living it up, parties, or sex. How would you wish to spend your last week on earth?

In times like these we need to do some serious thinking and planning for the future. You may have more than a week of life yet. Perhaps a year or a few years, but what then? The night is truly far spent. On our campuses there is lawlessness and unrest. In our cities there is rioting and rebellion. Millions of people are disillusioned. They do not know which way to go. They try to bolster their courage by taking a shot of liquor or heroin or speed. I heard a young man the other day say, "I know speed kills. My mother died an alcoholic and I am hooked on drugs. I wish I knew how to lick it." To this young man and to countless others I would like to say that you need a Saviour.

My wife and our friend, Paul Sharpe, saw a man commit suicide one time in the Tyne River

in England. We saw him go down and he was lost
to sight in those muddy waters. A police launch
sought to save him, but in vain. An hour later he
was dredged up from the bottom of the river, but
he was dead. If only someone could have saved
him. We could not. Why did he want to end his
life? If only he could have known the One who
came to give us the better life, the best in life,
he might have lived to make the world a brighter,
a better place. Is there anyone who can help us,
one who understands our hearts, when the thorns
of life have pierced them till they bleed; one who
sympathizes with us, who in wondrous love imparts
just the very, very blessing that we need?

> Yes, there's one, only One,
> The Blessed, Blessed Jesus,
> He's the One!
> When afflictions press the soul,
> When waves of trouble roll,
> And you need a friend to help you,
> He's the One.

The young man asked the way. Jesus is the Way.
This is a basic fact. Your great need is not freedom,
more money, a better job, or even security. You
need an anchor, you need a Saviour. The words
of this hymn describe your need so well, and the
way to fill that need.

> In times like these you need a Saviour,
> In times like these you need an anchor,
> Be very sure, be very sure,
> Your anchor holds, and grips the Solid Rock.

> This Rock is Jesus,
> Yes, He's the One,
> This Rock is Jesus,
> The only One.
> Be very sure, be very sure,
> Your anchor holds,
> And grips the Solid Rock.

In times like these you need the Bible,
In times like these, oh be not idle:
Be very sure, be very sure,
Your anchor holds,
And grips the solid Rock.

In times like these I have a Saviour,
In times like these I have an anchor,
I'm very sure, I'm very sure,
My anchor holds, and grips the solid Rock.

The Everlasting Arms

That heart cheering promise found in Deuteronomy 33:27, "The Eternal God is thy refuge, and underneath are the everlasting arms," has proved a soothing balm and a downy pillow to many a weary soul and sorrow-stricken man or woman. Just to know He is there, and that He cares, just to know that when all other helpers fail, when you have sunken to the bottom of despair; even there is the Eternal God, and underneath your despair are the Everlasting Arms. This is like cool water to a thirsty soul, and comfort indeed from Him who is the God of all comfort.

The Reverend Anthony J. Showalter found it so in Georgia and Alabama in 1888. He had been conducting singing classes and Bible study groups and revival services in South Carolina, Georgia and Alabama. While in an Alabama town he received two letters from two friends whom he had met in South Carolina while holding services there. Both men were grief stricken because they had recently lost their wives. The wife of each had died within a day or two of the other. Trying to find some way to comfort these two men by letter, the scripture found in Deuteronomy 33:27 came to his mind. While writing the letter he tried to recall some hymn based on the Everlasting Arms and could not think of one. It was then he decided to compose a hymn using these comforting words of promise.

He sat down at the piano and composed the music and the words of the chorus came to him readily. However, he was unable to write any suitable verses to go with the chorus.

> Leaning, leaning, safe and secure from all
>   alarms,
> Leaning, leaning, leaning on the Everlasting
>   Arms.

The Rev. Showalter sent his music and the chorus to another minister from his native Pennsylvania, the Rev. Elisha A. Hoffman, author of the hymn, I Must Tell Jesus. In a brief note he asked Mr. Hoffman to please put suitable words to his music and retain the theme of his chorus, if possible. Mr. Hoffman liked the music, and wrote the words as they are now sung. He returned the new hymn to Mr. Showalter, who sang the hymn for the first time at the Pine Log Methodist Church, in Pine Log, Georgia.

> What a fellowship, what a joy divine,
> Leaning on the Everlasting Arms;
> What a blessedness, what a peace is mine,
> Leaning on the Everlasting Arms.

A revival service held by Rev. Showalter brought many people to know the Lord Jesus Christ as their personal Saviour at Pine Log Methodist Church. Two years before these services another evangelist had held services here in 1886. On the evening of August 31, 1886, the evangelist, J. H. Sullivan, was disappointed with the seeming indifference of the congregation. The Rev. Sullivan prayed for the

Lord to shake the church if it took that to awaken the people. Almost immediately the church and surrounding community was shaken by an earthquake. Then many members of the congregation fell on their knees begging God for mercy.

A marker erected in front of a new church on the old site commemorates that memorable earthquake revival. I have written to the present pastor of the church asking for further information about the marker.

> Oh, how sweet to walk in this pilgrim way,
> Leaning on the Everlasting Arms;
> Oh, how bright the path grows from day to
>   day,
> Leaning on the Everlasting Arms.

Elisha A. Hoffman was born in Orwigsburg, Pennsylvania, May 7, 1837. He was the son of a minister and decided to follow in his father's footsteps. He was licensed to preach in 1886, the same year as the earthquake at Pine Log, Georgia. One of Mr. Hoffman's first hymns was Glory to His Name, also known as Down at the Cross. Perhaps the Rev. Hoffman's most beloved hymn is I Must Tell Jesus. For the touching story surrounding his writing of this hymn see the story I wrote on I Must Tell Jesus.

> What have I to dread, what have I to fear?
> Leaning on the Everlasting Arms;
> I have blessed peace, with my Lord so near,
> Leaning on the Everlasting Arms.

It is not uncommon for people to die from fear and worry. A dread of the unknown has haunted many a man and woman to an untimely grave. What a joy divine, leaning on the Everlasting Arms. You too can know this peace that passes understanding. Seek the Lord today, for He has said,

"Those that seek me early shall find me." (Prov. 8:17).

Beneath the Cross of Jesus

The story of the crucifixion is this world's most beautiful love story. To think that Jesus Christ, the Creator of all things, the Mighty God, would love you and me so much that He would willingly die for us. Not just a common death, but that cruel suffering of the cross. Herein is love. Not that we loved Him, but that He loved us and gave Himself for us. "Behold what love the Father hath bestowed upon us, that we should be called the sons of God. And it doth not yet appear what we shall be. But we know that when He shall appear we shall be like Him." (I John 3:1-2).

> Beneath the Cross of Jesus
> I fain would take my stand—
> The shadow of a mighty Rock
> Within a weary land;
> A home within the wilderness,
> A rest upon the way,
> From the burning of the noontide heat,
> And the burden of the day.

Every true folower of the Lord Jesus Christ at some time in his Christian experience wishes to take his stand there beneath the cross. There at the Cross where my burdens rolled away, and where I found grace to cover all my sins, there I return for strength and grace to help in time of need. That Mighty Rock within a weary land is none other than the Saviour Himself. He not only is a shelter from the blazing heat, but He is the One who took my burden and slipped into the yoke beside me. That is why His yoke is easy, it is not heavy, it does not hurt me. He is carrying the load. We are there together, my Lord and I, but I have learned to cast my burden upon Him and He sustains me. He would willingly bear your burden too.

> Upon that cross of Jesus
> Mine eye at times can see
> The very dying form of One
> Who suffered there for me;
> And from my smitten heart with tears
> Two wonders I confess—
> The wonders of redeeming love
> And my unworthiness.

Time after time the believer can go back to that cross where he first saw the Light and get another glimpse of the very dying form of One who suffered there for him. Oh, the wonder of it all! My sins are all nailed to His cross. My name is written in the nail prints in His hands. (Isa. 49:15). Why did He love us so? Love so amazing, so divine, demands my life, my love, my all.

> I take, O cross, thy shadow
> For my abiding place;
> I ask no other sunshine than
> The sunshine of His face;
> Content to let the world go by,
> To know no gain nor loss,
> My sinful self my only shame,
> My glory all the cross.

When His face shines upon you it is joy unspeakable. This is taking a trip without pill or needle. This is Beulah Land. This is heaven. There are no serious reactions when one takes Jesus into His heart. There is no remorse, no regret. It is joy, and life and peace. St. Paul spoke lovingly of his experience with that cross. He said: "I am crucified with Christ, nevertheless I live, yet not I, but

Christ liveth in me. And the life that I now live in the flesh, I live by the faith of the Son of God, who loved me, and gave Himself for me." (Gal. 2:20). When we can so identify ourselves with Christ and with His cross, that we are crucified with Him; then we can truly say, not I but Christ. Christ liveth in me. Oh, what a salvation this, Christ liveth in me!

This beautiful hymn was written by Elizabeth Clephane, author of The Ninety and Nine. Elizabeth Clephane was born in Edinburgh, Scotland, June 18, 1830. Her sister wrote to Ira Sankey, the famous Gospel singer: "My sister was a very quiet little child, shrinking from notice and was always absorbed in books. The loss of both her parents at an early age taught her sorrow. As she grew up she was recognized as the cleverest one of our family. She was first in her class and a favorite in school. Her love for poetry was a passion. Among the sick and suffering she won the name, "My Sunbeam." She wrote The Ninety and Nine for a friend, who had it published in *The Children's Hour*. It was copied from this into many publications, but was comparatively little noticed. She died in 1869. She was only 39."

In my book, *Next Hymn Story, Please!* I have told the story of the hymn, The Ninety and Nine. I quote, "D. L. Moody and Ira Sankey were holding revival meetings in Edinburgh. One day, while riding on a train together, Mr. Sankey was reading a newspaper, hoping to find some American news. He closed the paper and then upon reopening it he saw the poem on the Good Shepherd. He was so impressed with the poem, he read it to Mr. Moody. But Mr. Moody was lost in thought and made no comment. The following evening Mr.

Moody preached on the Good Shepherd; then he
asked Mr. Horatious Bonar to make an appeal.
He then asked Mr. Sankey if he had anything ap-
propriate to sing. Mr. Sankey thought he had nothing. Then the Lord seemed to say: "Sing the hymn
you clipped from the newspaper today." But there
was no music. Without doubting God, Mr. Sankey
sat down at the organ and began to compose a
tune as the Lord dictated it to his heart. He sang
the first verse, but what was he to do on the second?
Could he remember the notes well enough to play
them again? That would have been impossible
had not God whispered them to his heart.

"The hymn finished, Mr. Moody came to Mr.
Sankey in tears, and asked: 'Where did you get
that hymn? It was the most beautiful thing I have
ever heard.' Sankey replied that it was the one
he had read to him on the train earlier in the day.

"I should like to recount here the story of two
men who were converted through this hymn. Mr.
Sankey relates that 'at the close of our meetings
in Newcastle-on-Tyne, one of the most efficient
workers in our meetings, Mrs. Claphin, decided
to go to the Continent for a season of rest. When
passing through London she purchased a number
of the cheapest edition of *Sacred Songs and Solos*,
for free distribution on the way. At the Grand Hotel
in Paris she left a number of them on the reading
table with a prayer for God's blessing upon those
who might find them there. A few weeks later she
attended a prayer meeting in Geneva. The minister
of the church told a touching story about a young
English lady who was a member of his church.
She received a letter from a long-lost brother, who
was ill in the Grand Hotel in Paris. The young
lady asked her physician if he would allow her to

go to Paris to visit her brother. The physician said, 'You will die if you do.' She replied, 'I will die if I don't.' On reaching the Grand Hotel she was taken to the room where her dying brother lay. After a warm welcome, he took from under his pillow a copy of *Sacred Songs and Solos,* pointing to The Ninety and Nine, he said, 'This hymn was the means of bringing me to Christ.' Mrs. Claphin thanked God for putting it into her heart to distribute the little hymn books.'

"Miss Clephane did not live to hear either of her hymns sung or to know they had been such a blessing. They were both put to music several years after her death. Jesus Himself said: 'The Good Shepherd giveth His life for the sheep.' 'There were ninety and nine that safely lay, in the shelter of the fold. But one was out on the hill away, far from the gates of gold.' That lost one is you. The Shepherd went out to find you, to bring you safely home. 'But none of the ransomed ever knew how deep were the waters crossed; nor how dark was the night that the Lord passed through, e're He found His sheep that was lost.' My sinful self my only shame, my glory all the cross.

"God forbid that I should glory, save in the cross of our Lord Jesus Christ, by whom the world is crucified unto me and I unto the world."

Jesus Loves Me!

He was small, he was dirty and he was a bit wild. He came running to me as I entered a tennament house. "Say, Mister, do you love me?" he asked, with a sheepish grin. "I sure do," I replied. I put my arm around his shoulders and he sort

of melted against me. "Can I go home with you?"
he asked, with a pleading tone. I told him his mother could never get along without him. He curled
up his lip and said: "She's at the bars." They called
him Don Don. It may have been a real name. It
may have been a nickname. One thing was sure,
Don Don wanted someone to love him. Later his
mother brought him to us, with his meager supply
of clothes, and we kept Don Don for several weeks.
Those were happy days for that little fellow, perhaps the only happy part of his life. His mother
wanted us to keep him. London was being pounded
with V1 and V2 bombs. We had to return to help
our people in London. We could not take Don Don
into that holocaust. Perhaps we made a mistake.
Should we have taken him? We left him to go back
to the streets. I am sorry we did that. We never
saw him again. We did love him, and he learned
that Jesus loves him.

Now about a young lady of 21. She looked much
younger, she was so thin, so pale. Her grandmother,
Mrs. Oliver, asked me to visit her dear bairnie.
She called her Bonnie. She was a bit of Scotland
living in Newcastle-on-Tyne. Bonnie was a con-
sumptive. She coughed quite a bit when we visited
her. She was seldom out of bed. But she had a
radiance about her that was not of this world. The
last time Mrs. Konkel and I saw Bonnie was just
before we left for London. She was disturbed to
hear we were going away. "We shall return soon,"
I told her. But she could not wait. She died calling
for us a few days later. Before we left Bonnie she
said, "I want to sing." I said, "Good, what shall
we sing?" She said, "Jesus Loves Me, This I
Know." She then said, "I want to sit up." She was
not strong enough to sit alone. I took her hand and

helped her. Her voice was weak but sweet:

> Jesus loves me! this I know,
> For the Bible tells me so;
> Little ones to Him belong,
> They are weak, but He is strong.

We sang with her but it was hard to keep back the tears as she continued on the third verse:

> Jesus loves me! loves me still,
> Tho' I'm very weak and ill;
> From His shining home on high,
> Comes to watch me where I lie.

Singing the hymn exhausted her and she sank back on the pillows. She truly belonged to Him. She wanted to get well, but she seemed to know she would not. She was planning on seeing Jesus soon. She did not have long to wait. A few days and she was with Him. Heaven's gates opened wide and Jesus Himself took her home on high.

This hymn was written by Anna Bartlett Warner. She was born at Westpoint, New York, in the year 1820. With her younger sister she helped write several stories, the best known of which was *The Wide Wide World.* Her sister was a year younger than Anna. Susan, or Susanne, wrote the children's hymn,

> Jesus bids us shine
> With a pure, clear light.

Anna wrote other hymns including, One More Day's Work for Jesus, and We Would See Jesus. Miss Warner wrote this simple little hymn for her Sunday school children. She taught a Sunday school class and wrote a new hymn for them occasionally. Anna used Amy Lothrop as a pen name. She died near the spot where she was born at the advanced age of ninety-five. Her hymn, Jesus Loves

Me, has gone around the world.

A missionary among the Hindus in Southern India wrote an interesting story in connection with this hymn. He translated the words into Telugu and taught the hymn to his day school children. He was going through town a week later when he heard one of the boys from his school singing this hymn to a group of men and women who stopped to hear.

"Sonny, where did you learn that song?" someone asked. "Over at the missionary school," he replied. "Who is Jesus? and what is the Bible?" was the next question. "Jesus is the name of Him who came into the world to save us from our sins, and the Bible is the book from God. That is what the missionaries taught me." Truly, a little child shall lead them.

I had a refreshing experience with this hymn out in Africa. I was going through a Moslem village. A young man who opposed my taking a picture of two wild pigs, "because you must pay money," later invited me to speak to the people of the village. About thirty people were gathered together in the shade. A chair was brought for me and I was told to proceed. I asked how many knew Jesus. The young man who forbid me to take pictures of the pigs asked me, "Who He?" Two people in the group said they had heard of Jesus. One said he heard a man mention His name in Monrovia years ago. He had forgotten the particulars. It may have been an open-air meeting. He had heard the name, but he did not know who Jesus is. A woman too said she had heard of Jesus. She thought He was a great man. She had forgotten where He lived. She thought it was in Africa.

I realized I was with a group of people who

would hear about their Saviour for the first time. Offering up a silent prayer for God to guide me, I told them of the Good Shepherd, who loved them and gave Himself for them. I asked if they liked to sing. They all answered yes. Most Africans love to sing and are natural harmonizers. I taught them the words of Jesus Loves Me. We sang it over and over. They loved it. I told them: "Jesus loves every one of you. He died to save you, and to forgive your sins. Will you give your hearts to Him? He will come into your heart if you will let Him." When I asked how many would like to have Jesus in their hearts, almost every hand went up. I left them with a prayer that God would honor His Word and save them for Jesus' sake. It was a thrilling experience. I often wonder whether I will see any of that little group of Africans in heaven.

> Jesus loves me, He who died,
> Heaven's gates to open wide;
> He will wash away my sin,
> Let His little child come in.

This hymn exalts the Saviour and is a story of Jesus and His love. The trend of some clergy and churchmen is to minimize the power and authority of Jesus. God's Word says there is no other Saviour. Jesus Himself said, "I am the Way, the Truth, and the Life, no man cometh unto the Father but by me." When Jehoshaphat went out with Ahab to battle, the enemy soldiers were told: "Fight with none but with the king." The captains especially were to shoot only at the king. Today there are those who are shooting at the King of Kings, the Lord Jesus Christ. They discount His divinity, His authority, His Word. Jesus said, "Without me ye can do nothing."

Young people today do not dig the scholarly sermons that discuss social injustice but ignore the Saviour. Love, the love of Jesus they understand. Like little Don Don they want to be loved, they want to belong. Do you want Him as your Saviour? Then ask Him to come into your heart, and He will.

Jesus Loves Even Me

Have you ever reached the place where you thought you were forsaken by both man and God? If you have had that experience, as many others, then this little message may be especially for you. God so loved the world that He gave Jesus to be your Saviour. Jesus so loves the world today that He is still calling the lost, the hopeless, the wretched and the sinful to himself. He does more than stand at the door and call, as we read in Revelation 3:20. He goes out to seek the lost. If you have ever felt downhearted and forsaken, or if you feel now that you are alone in the world, just remember Jesus loves even you. Turn to John 3:16, 6:37, and Isaiah 53:5-6 and read these scriptures for yourself.

Philip Bliss was born in the mountain region near Rome, Pennsylvania, July 9, 1838. His parents were farmers who were very poor. From the time he was a small child he loved music. He tried to make flutes from the reeds that grew near his father's house. On occasion he was allowed to go to town to sell vegetables door-to-door to help augment the family income. This he loved to do. When he was ten, he went to town one Saturday with his basket of vegetables. It was a warm, sunny day and he had no shoes. From the open door of a house he heard music. He walked into the house and saw a lady playing the piano. Not wishing to disturb her, and not realizing how wrong it was to enter a house without an invitation, he went over to the piano. The lady looked up, horrified. She saw a young boy with large patches on his overalls, and, of all things, bare feet! She shouted, "You get out of here with your great bare feet!" The lad burst into tears because the music he so loved was denied him.

When Philip was a young lad of sixteen he was converted. Because of his love for music he began to devote as much time as he could spare to it. At the age of nineteen he attended a musical convention in Rome, Pennsylvania, where he met Mr. William Bradbury who encouraged him to study hymnody. Some of the hymns that he gave the world are "Whosoever Will," "Hold the Fort," "Almost Persuaded," "Man of Sorrows," and "I Am So Glad that Our Father in Heaven."

Mr. Bliss met D. L. Moody in Chicago about the year 1869. Mr. Moody was impressed with the sweetness of his voice and its range and quality. He was also impressed with the young man's saintly life. Soon after this, Mr. Moody went to Scotland, and from Glasgow he wrote a letter to Philip Bliss, urging him to obey the call of God and enter full-time evangelistic work. Mr. Ira Sankey, the hymnwriter who conducted the hymn singing for Moody, tells of a prayer meeting he attended soon after this letter reached Bliss. Bliss spoke of the letter at the prayer meeting. He was facing a decision. The Handel and Haydn Society of San Francisco had offered him a lucrative position. At that prayer meeting he decided for Christ. "In simple, childlike, trusting prayer, he placed himself at the disposal of the Lord."

> I am so glad that our Father in Heaven,
> Tells of His love in the Book He has given;
> Wonderful things in the Bible I see;
> This is the dearest, that Jesus loves me.
> > I am so glad that Jesus loves me,
> > Jesus loves even me.

This hymn was written in June 1870, some time after Mr. Bliss had received Moody's letter from Glasgow. He wrote the hymn to bring out the truth of Romans 5:5: "The love of God is shed abroad in our hearts." He had heard a congregation singing "Oh, How I Love Jesus," and the thought occurred to him that we should be thinking more about His love for us.

A young woman in Dundee, Scotland, later heard Mr. Sankey sing "Jesus Loves Even Me." During the singing of the hymn she began to feel conviction for her sins for the first time. She saw that she was without Christ and lost. She went home but could not sleep. "Jesus cannot love me," she thought. "He could not love a sinner such as I." The next night she was one of the first to give her heart to Christ when the invitation was given. Then she, too, sang with all her heart, "Jesus Loves Even Me."

Oh, if there's only one song I can sing,
  When in His beauty I see the great King,
This shall my song through eternity be,
  Oh, what a wonder, that Jesus loves me!

Another young lady in Dundee told Mr. Sankey how God had used this hymn and her baby daughter to win her husband to Christ. The young mother was a true Christian. She had heard Mr. Sankey sing and she had taught her three-year-old daughter to sing "I am so glad that our Father in heaven." But about all she could remember was "Jesus loves me, Jesus loves even me." The mother tried to prevail upon her husband to go to the meetings, but he refused. One evening when he returned from work, his little daughter met him at the door. She threw her arms about him when he picked her up, and repeating her hymn, she said, "Daddy, Jesus loves even me. He loves even you." The father's heart was touched and tears filled his eyes. The Holy Spirit through a little child had accomplished what the mother and other friends had been unable to do. The father attended the meetings and gave his heart to Jesus.

Another story is told of a traveling salesman who attended the Moody-Sankey meetings in the City Hall of Glasgow. He later said that he was passing down Stockwell Street when he heard some people singing "I am so glad that Jesus loves me." "The words struck me," he said. "I felt as if a load was passing from my heart. I put my faith in that love and found peace. 'Yes,' I said to myself, 'though all the devils in hell try to move me from it, I will trust in the love that Jesus has had for me.'"

There is much more I should like to say about Mr. Bliss' other hymns, but space is limited. On December 29, 1876, Mr. and Mrs. Bliss were traveling on a train from Ohio to Chicago. There was a faulty bridge and the train was wrecked. Mr. Bliss got out of a window, but on hearing that his wife was trapped in the flames inside he went back to rescue her. They both lost their lives and were buried at Rome, Pennsylvania. The simple marker at the grave reads—"P. P. Bliss, Author of 'Hold the Fort.'"

There Is a Green Hill Far Away

The Irish people are great lovers of song. Wherever you see a group, you will eventually hear them pour out their hearts in the songs of the Emerald Isle. It has been suggested that most of their songs are of a sad nature, written in a minor key. Although this may be true of their folk and secular songs, it is not true of their hymns.

Few realize that "Jesus Calls Us O'er the Tumult," "Once in Royal David's City," "What a Friend We Have in Jesus," and "I've Wandered Far Away from God" were by Irish authors. Mrs. Alexander, Joseph Scriven, and William Kirkpatrick were all born in Northern Ireland; Thomas Kelly was born in Dublin. While in Ireland some time ago, I had the great pleasure of doing research work on these hymnwriters.

Much that has been written about the hymn "There is a Green Hill Far Away" and its author has proven to be false. I have been careful to seek out the true story and believe our readers will appreciate the facts. One book in my possession states that Mrs. Cecil Frances Alexander wrote this hymn to teach some boys in her Sunday school class the truth of the creed and help them to understand better the catechism. The words crucified, dead and buried had little meaning to the children. It is said that Mrs. Alexander lived near Londonderry, and frequently went to that city for shopping. On these trips she passed the hill above the city, which reminded her of the hill Calvary.

I visited the house where Mrs. Alexander was born and where she wrote "There is a Green Hill Far Away." Milltown House is part of a large country estate on a hill above Strabane. The house was occupied by Mrs. Harpur and her son, Major Harpur, with his wife, and her daughter-in-law and son-in-law, Mr. and Mrs. Wallace, of the Colonial Office. I met true Irish hospitality there, and everywhere I went seeking information.

"There is a Green Hill Far Away" was written in 1848 by Miss C. F. Humphreys, two years before her marriage to Reverend Alexander. It seems quite clear that her shopping expeditions would have been to Strabane and not to Londonderry. The hill that Miss Humphreys no doubt had in mind when she wrote the hymn was Knockavoe Hill, on the estate adjoining the one where she was born. She played on this hill as a child and loved it. When viewed from a distance, the hill has a slight resemblance to the shape of a skull.

Mr. and Mrs. Wallace took me to Donegal to visit a niece of Mrs. Alexander, Mrs. John Taylor. Although nearly eighty, she was at the time in good health and active mentally. She had many beautiful memories of her aunt. She thought that the favorite of all her aunt's hymns was "Jesus Calls Us O'er the Tumult." This hymn is perhaps better known in America than "Once in Royal David's City" or "All Things Bright and Beautiful," both of which are often sung by children.

Mrs. Taylor recalled once having heard a Catholic priest praise the hymn "There is a Green Hill Far Away." He declared that "It was written by Bishop Cecil Frances Alexander, who was an ardent Irish Catholic." This amused those Protestants present who knew Mrs. Alexander personally after her husband had been consecrated Bishop (Protestant).

Before she was married, Miss Humphreys did all in her power to help the poor children in her Sunday school class as well as their parents. She made endless visits to their homes, sewing, cooking, mending, and caring for the sick, the aged and the infirm. This she continued to do throughout her life. She consistently refused to accept for her own use any royalties for her writings. Any money that was sent her was given to an Irish school for the deaf.

The French composer, Charles Gounod, wrote a beautiful tune for "There is a Green Hill Far Away." His little daughter had come back from boarding school in England where she had memorized many hymns. When she recited this one to her father, he thought it so beautiful that he immediately composed the tune which is so commonly sung to Mrs. Alexander's words.

The hymns "All Things Bright and Beautiful" and "Once in Royal David's City" are often sung by children, as stated previously, the world over. A trusting child of God does not doubt that God made the tiny dewdrops and the "purple-headed mountain"; that He painted the rose and made "all creatures great and small"; that He "died to save us all." It is only after sin has hardened the heart that man begins to doubt and deny the Saviour who was born "in royal David's city."

In these lines Mrs. Alexander tells us in simple and

beautiful words the way of salvation:

> O dearly, dearly has He loved,
>   And we must love Him too.
> And trust in His redeeming blood,
>   And try His works to do.

All Things Bright and Beautiful

This beautiful hymn, and many of the other hymns
by Mrs. Alexander, were written for the children of her
Sunday school class to teach them the various truths
contained in the Apostle's Creed. "There is a Green Hill
Far Away" was written to illustrate: "Suffered under
Pontius Pilate, was crucified, dead and buried." "All
Things Bright and Beautiful" was written to illustrate:
"I believe in God, the Father Almighty, Maker of heaven
and earth."

It was my privilege on one occasion to visit Milltown
House, near Strabane, Northern Ireland, where this
hymn was written. Cecil Frances Humphreys was born
in 1823; the daughter of Major and Mrs. John Humphreys. Cecil lived at Milltown House until shortly before
she married Rev. William Alexander, who later became
Primate of all Ireland.

> All things bright and beautiful,
> All creatures great and small,
> All things wise and wonderful,
> The Lord God made them all.

It is indeed wonderful to see how a child of God will
trust implicitly in Jesus, who made all things bright and
beautiful. He will not doubt that the Saviour who made
the tiny dewdrop and the purple-headed mountain, also
made all creatures great and small. It seems that it is
only when sin creeps into the heart that man begins to

doubt the Creator. It was King David who sang of the
beauty of the heavens and the earth in the Eighth Psalm.
"When I consider Thy heavens, the work of Thy fingers,
the moon and the stars, which thou hast ordained, what
is man, that thou art mindful of him? and the Son of
man, that thou visitest him?" How can one look at the
stars and the moon, consider their beauty, their distance
from the earth, and doubt the Creator who made them
all? On occasion I have been amazed at the beauty in a
fly's wing or the foot of a spider, when they are placed under the microscope. Why did God clothe the butterfly in
such a gorgeous array of colors? Did He not make all the
beauties of nature for man to enjoy?

> Each little flower that opens,
> Each little bird that sings,
> He made their glowing colors,
> He made their tiny wings.
>
> The purple-headed mountain
> The river running by,
> The sunset and the morning
> That brightens up the sky.

After her marriage, Mrs. Alexander moved to Londonderry with her husband, where he became Bishop of
Derry and Primate of all Ireland. Londonderry is a
walled city, and on one occasion a friend, Miss Anna
Duddy, took me to the city and we actually walked on
top of the walls, and recounted the story of the thirteen
apprentice boys who cried, "No Surrender!" and so
heroically defied King James II and his armies. Later we
were thrilled as we watched 150 bands from all over Ireland and Scotland take part in a great parade and
demonstrations commemorating the relief of Derry.

We need people today who will courageously stand up
for Jesus, and defy the forces of evil and the enemy of all
righteousness. Determine in your heart that you will help
to make the place where you live a better and more beautiful place because you dared to do what is right.

The cold wind in the winter,
The pleasant summer sun,
The ripe fruits in the garden,
He made them every one.

He gave us eyes to see them,
And lips that we might tell
How great is God Almighty,
Who hath done all things well.

Do you ever remember to thank God for your eyes? Did you ever think to thank God that you can hear and speak? I had a friend in London who was a deaf mute. He could not remember ever having heard a sound in all his life. He taught me to speak with my hands in sign language, and he used to tell me how he would love to be able to hear the birds and the voices of little children in laughter.

Mrs. Alexander went into the homes of the poor and brought cheer and joy to many in need. Never did people feel that she was lowering herself to visit them. They could feel that she was their friend. She was truly their friend, because she knew the Friend of sinners, who made all things bright and beautiful.

I want to see Jesus someday, don't you? To see Jesus is the major goal and ambition of my life. What a grand and glorious day that will be, when we step into the presence of the King of Kings, who made and loved us all, and hear Him say, "Well done, thou good and faithful servant, enter thou into the joy of thy Lord." Do you want to see Jesus too? Then ask Him just now to come into your heart and make you pure and clean, and to cleanse you from all sin, and He will.

Dare To Be a Daniel

"You wouldn't dare." Those words have been repeated many, many times, prompted by fear or danger. Sometimes a young person is given a dare, or asked to do something that is wrong. If he or she refuses, he is branded as "chicken" or "yellow." People admire the boy or girl, man or woman, who will dare to stand up for his principles, even though his principles may hazard his popularity, his job, or even his life.

Doctor Bob Pierce told this very touching story: "A story I shall never forget was told to me by a missionary named Jim Dickson as we walked down a winding mountain trail in Formosa. Jim was pointing out that as recently as 1932 the aborigines practiced headhunting on the island. The heads were offered in heathen sacrifices to their heathen gods. 'What was it that caused these people to abandon headhunting?' I asked Jim. In reply Jim said that it was Christianity that changed the hearts of the people. This is the way it came about. 'Gow Hong was a little old Chinese merchant from the lowlands of Formosa. Gow came up here first to trade with the aborigines. He sold them salt and other things they could not produce for themselves. Eventually he came to live among them, and taught them the ways of the true God. They could see that he loved them. He told them that headhunting was wrong, and pleaded with them not to kill any more people and take their heads for sacrifice. They thought over what he told them, and after much discussion among themselves, they came to Gow Hong and said, "We have decided to take only a few heads this year." Gow told them that "a few is too many." After a day or two they came back and said, "We will only take one head this year for sacrifice." Gow insisted, "No heads," but they held out for one. When they would not

give in, Gow asked them where they were to hold their
sacrifice. Trusting him, they revealed how they would
wait for a dark night and catch their victim along a lone-
ly path near a neighboring warring tribe.

" 'On the night appointed, everything was prepared
in the woods for the heathen sacrifice. They waited in
breathless silence for their victim to come along the wil-
derness path. As they waited their excitement grew. As
the hour approached midnight they heard footsteps.
They pounced on their victim and a sharp knife prevent-
ed him from screaming or struggling. They severed his
head and put it in a basket. They returned to their place
of sacrifice, and when they removed the head from the
basket, in the light of the fire, there were piercing cries,
then silence. They had killed their friend, Gow Hong!
They had said, "Just one more head"; Gow had sacri-
ficed his own to save another. When they saw they had
killed the only man who had ever cared for them, who
had tried to help them improve their own conditions,
they vowed, "There must never be another head sacri-
ficed." Gow Hong was willing to stand alone and by so
doing he won a tribe of headhunters. Many of those one-
time headhunting aborigines are faithful Christians
today.' "

> Standing by a purpose true,
> Heeding God's command,
> Honor them, the faithful few!
> All hail to Daniel's band.

> Dare to be a Daniel!
> Dare to stand alone!
> Dare to have a purpose firm!
> Dare to make it known!

Some years ago, in the city of London, I read a little
book by two British missionaries who went to China.
They were Mildred Cable and Francisca French. The
book was called *Through Jade Gate.* I quote: "Visiting in

our city we soon learned that the most difficult plough-
ing was being done by the children. Everywhere we were
welcomed, and mothers whom we had never seen before
quoted Scripture texts, hymns and sentences of prayers
with surprising accuracy. One little fellow, unconscious
that he was being watched, walked down the street, singing at the top of his voice, 'Dare to be a Daniel, dare to
stand alone.' Coming to a stop in front of a peanut ven-
dor and looking him in the face, he said, 'Did you know
that there is only one God and one Lord Jesus Christ?'
'Why, no, I did not,' said the man bewildered. 'Well, it is
true,' announced the child, and passed on down the
street, continuing 'Dare to have a purpose firm, dare to
make it known.' "

An Excellent Spine

When I visit Dublin, Ireland, I love to go into the library at Trinity College and look at the fine display of
old Bibles there. There are many old translations which
have some peculiar, and sometimes humorous, errors in
spelling. They are called printer's errors or typographical
errors. There is one translation which describes Joseph
as being a "lucky fellow." The King James Version says
he was a "prosperous man" (Gen. 39:2). Another translation describes Daniel as being tops, thus: "Then this
Daniel was preferred above the presidents and princes,
because *an excellent spine* was in him: and the King
thought to set him over the whole realm." The King
James Version says that "an *excellent spirit* was in
him." But, never mind, it took an excellent spine or
backbone to stand up for God in the face of death as
Daniel did. When he was thrown into the den of lions, the
lions purred around him like kittens. Not one of those
fierce lions tried to harm Daniel. God shut the lions'
mouths. Some boys and girls, men and women, have lost
their lives daring to stand up for Christ. They were not

really lost. They said good-night to this dark world, and were welcomed by the Sun of Righteousness, where there is no more death.

"Him That Honoreth Me, I Will Honor."

Eric Liddell was one of the world's fastest runners back in the 1920's. He was a young Scotsman. Eric was chosen to represent Scotland at the Olympic Games in Paris. He was to run the 100 meter dash. Little did Eric realize what it would mean when he made the greatest decision of his life, to take Christ as his Saviour.

He arrived in Paris with the rest of the English team and went to look at the schedule. To his dismay, the 100 meter dash was to be run on a Sunday. Eric was stunned. The thought came to him, "When in Rome, do as the Romans do." But another voice seemed to protest, "No, when in Rome, do as you would at home." He found a quiet place and cried out his heart to God in prayer. After prayer, it was settled. He would not dishonor his Lord and His day. The newspapers took up the story and pointed out what a prude Eric was, that he was letting Scotland down, since he was their only hope of taking a world record. Eric's popularity waned very low.

Then Eric noticed that the 400 meter dash would not be run on Sunday. He went to the manager and asked for permission to run the 400. He had never practiced that distance. As he went out to the starting point, someone placed a small piece of paper in his hand. It read, "Him that honoreth Me, I will honor." He won the race and established a world record. The "spoil-sport" was carried off the field shoulder-high.

Eric heard the call to go to China as a missionary. During the war he was interned and died for his Saviour in a concentration camp.

Do you have the courage to stand up for Christ? You can, if you will ask Him to forgive your sins and come into your heart just now. Will you dare to stand for Him, who loved you, and gave himself for you?

> Many giants, great and tall,
> Stalking through the land,
> Headlong to the earth would fall,
> If met by Daniel's band.

Dare to be a Daniel; dare to stand alone!

Stand Up For Jesus

No doubt you have all joined in singing the lovely hymn, "Stand Up! Stand Up for Jesus." You may know how to sing the hymn, but do you know what it means to really and truly do what the hymn says—to stand up for Jesus? Young people learn very early to stand up for their rights, and some are far too forward at that. Most of you will stand up for your children. You would not let anyone say anything against them. The soldiers that fight for their country in war are standing up for their country. A Christian must be just as brave as a soldier in war, and must have even more courage.

How To Be a Christian Soldier

Now, if you are going to stand up for Jesus properly, you will have to first take Him into your heart. When you have Jesus in your heart, you love Him, and when you love Him more than anyone or anything else in the world, it is easy to stand up for Him.

But how can people take Jesus into their hearts and love Him? Well, it is really very easy for young people, but sometimes very hard for older people. You have all done something that you felt sorry about. Did you ever disobey God's commands? Did you ever tell a lie or steal anything? If you have done any of these things, you are a

sinner, and must have Jesus forgive you. Just tell Him in
a simple prayer that you have done wrong, tell Him what
it was, and tell Him how sorry you are about it. Tell Him
you are ashamed you have done these things. Then ask
our heavenly Father to forgive you for Jesus' sake.
Acknowledge that Jesus died for you, and that you are
going to take Him into your heart and live for Him. Tell
your heavenly Father that you will stand up for Jesus.
Then ask those you have wronged to forgive you. When
you have done all that, tell the Lord you are ready to accept His salvation by faith and He will forgive you.
When God forgives you, you are a Christian.

> Stand up! stand up for Jesus,
>   Ye soldiers of the Cross!
> Lift high His royal banner,
>   It must not suffer loss.
> From vict'ry unto vict'ry
>   His army shall He lead,
> Till ev'ry foe is vanquished,
>   And Christ is Lord indeed.

This hymn was written because a preacher, who was
a true soldier of the Cross, sent word to the men of the
Young Men's Christian Association to "Stand up for
Jesus." The minister's name was the Rev. Dudley A.
Tang. When he sent this word, he was dying. He lost his
life in a very unusual way.

It happened about 100 years ago, in Philadelphia. In
those days they used donkeys to pull a long pole around
in a circle. The pole was attached to wheels that turned
to grind grain. It was a slow process, but it worked very
well.

Rev. Tang loved animals and he reached over to pet
the donkey's head. Just then one of the big cogs caught
his sleeve, and in a moment his arm was drawn right into
the cogs and was cut off.

Rev. Tang had preached in the Y.M.C.A. the Sunday
before. There were 5,000 men in the meeting, and 1,000 of
them were so much under conviction that they asked

God to forgive their sins and they became Christians in that meeting. Thousands of young men and women all over Philadelphia were going every day at noon and at night to pray and to seek the Lord. It was on Wednesday that the Rev. Tang lay dying of infection that, in those days, was not easily controlled. He could not go to preach to the young men that night, but he sent a message to them: "Stand up for Jesus!" The next day he died.

Another preacher, the Rev. George Duffield, was in the room when the dying man sent that message. He thought, "What a lovely message, a sermon in one sentence." The words kept going through his mind and God gave him a poem: it was this hymn.

Rev. Duffield preached the funeral sermon for his friend and told about his last message to the young men; then he read his poem. Perhaps no one else would ever have heard of that poem that we love so much to sing today, if it had not been for a Sunday school teacher. This teacher made several copies of the poem and taught it to the Sunday school children. A copy was given to a man who published a religious paper. Someone read it and set it to music, and now "Stand Up for Jesus" is sung almost all over the world, in many languages.

A Cripple and His Crutches

One time a young man who had been crippled for many years was listening to a radio program. He heard the congregation singing "Stand Up for Jesus." He wrote to Dr. S. Parkes Cadman and told him that he was in bed when the hymn was announced, but he was so impressed with it and the thought of his debt to his Saviour that, "When you sang 'Stand Up for Jesus,' I got out of bed and stood up with my crutches out of respect to my Master."

> Stand up! stand up for Jesus!
>   Stand in His strength alone;
> The arm of flesh will fail you;
>   Ye dare not trust your own.

Put on the gospel armor,
    Each piece put on with prayer;
Where duty calls, or danger,
    Be never wanting there.

To be a strong soldier for Jesus you will need to be pure and holy. When you love Jesus with all your soul, and with all your mind and strength, you have on this gospel armor and you are pure and holy. Read about the armor in Eph. 6:11-12.

Would you like to enlist in the army of the Lord today? Then do just as I have told you, and ask Jesus to forgive you, and to come into your heart, and to help you to love Him and live for Him. Then you, too, can be a true soldier of the Cross, and stand up for Jesus.

Yield Not to Temptation

One of the most difficult things for Christians to do is to resist temptation. A young woman told me that temptations plagued her until she was almost ashamed to attend church. She feared the accusing eyes of more mature Christians. There is no easy answer to how to resist temptation. Prayer is effective. A fine Christian friend of mine told me of his battle for years to overcome a certain temptation. He yielded time after time. Then one day he prayed: "Lord, I cannot cope with this sin. I belong to *you*—body, soul, and spirit. Please fill me so full with your grace that when this temptation comes, I can just turn to you and hand over that temptation to you. I will not accept it anymore." From that time he was able, by God's grace, to resist that temptation. That is a good example.

Too Weak to Live Christ

Saint Paul said, "For me to live is Christ, and to die

is gain" (Phil. 1:21). A young man told me he would like to be a Christian. He felt a great desire to serve Christ. As an afterthought he told me, "I am too wicked. Even if I became a Christian, I could never live a Christian life five minutes. I would fall back into the dregs of my sins." If this is your problem, too, as it is the experience of many, remember that you invited Christ into your heart, and asked Him to live His life in you. Seek Him again and again and cast all your care upon Him, for he careth for you. When you invite Christ into your heart, you can rely on Him to help you resist temptation. A hymn by William Cowper says, "Satan fears and trembles when he sees the weakest saint upon his knees."

Machine Guns and Trust in God

A young man in Hyde Park, London, was scoffing at my suggestion to put his trust in Jesus Christ. "What good is He when you are in danger?" At that moment a most unusual thing happened. Another man came up out of the crowd and asked to be able to say a word. He said, "I was on the shores of Dunkirk (in France) with this brave man. We were overpowered by a superior enemy. We had no guns, no tanks, no planes. He was on his knees, crying to God to let him see his mother before he died. God answered his prayer, and we were delivered by a miracle. God answered the prayers of many of us. He has reason to be brave." The first young man walked away. His sin was boasting, which is lying.

> Yield not to temptation, for yielding is sin,
> Each victory will help you some other to win.
> Fight manfully onward; dark passions subdue;
> Look ever to Jesus, He'll carry you through.

Yes, sin is a dangerous enemy. It is more dangerous to you than communism. Communism strives to destroy the faith of its people. Faith in Christ is subject to ridicule and censure. Some of the finest Christians in the world are, or have been, in Communist prisons. They, as much or more than you and I, are sorely tempted. There is a temptation to give up, to deny Christ. Yet, it is Christ in you, the hope of glory.

> Ask the Saviour to help you,
> Comfort, strengthen, and keep you;
> He is willing to aid you
> He will carry you through.

Millions of people in America and in Europe are determined not to be slaves to a foreign power. Yet, how many, many, are slaves to drugs, alcohol, tobacco, and other evils? Sin, indeed, is a disgrace to any people— that is yielding to sin. Temptation is not a sin. Yet, when you yield to temptation, and indulge in the sin to which you have been tempted, that is sin. The secret of deliverance from your temptation is in the refrain: "Ask the Saviour to help you, comfort, strengthen, and keep you; He is willing to aid you; He will carry you through." Peter cried to the Lord in his distress and Jesus saved him. Later, he yielded to temptation and denied his Lord. He wept bitterly, and our Lord forgave him. He hears your cry; He sees your tears of repentance; He forgives. Yet, He wills that I should be pure, clean and holy. Purity of heart and life is not a sign of weakness. Your temptation may be even greater because you are determined to remain clean and pure. Just remember you have the Saviour to help you. So many who are in despair because of their sins have no God and no hope. If only they would cry to Him like the thief on the cross did, He would hear them and deliver them. King David said: "This poor man cried, and the Lord heard him, and delivered him out of all his fears" (Ps. 34:6).

> To him that o'ercometh, God giveth a crown;
> Through faith we shall conquer, though often cast down;
> He, who is our Saviour, our strength will renew;
> Look ever to Jesus, He'll carry you through.

This hymn was written by Horatio R. Palmer. He said, "I am reverently thankful that God gave me the song, and has used it as a power for good. The song is an inspiration. I was at work on the dry subject of 'Theory' when the complete idea flashed upon my mind. I laid aside the theoretical work and hurriedly penned both words and music as fast as I could write them. I submitted it to a friend's criticism later, and some changes were made in the third stanza. The rest is exactly as it came to me from the Lord."

An incident regarding this hymn has to do with a women's prison in New York. Every Sunday afternoon the women were permitted to come out of their cells and sit in the corridor to hear a Christian lady talk, and to sing hymns with her. One day some of the women rebelled against an order of the matron, and a terrible scene followed. Screams, threats, and profanity filled the air. The matron hastily sent to the men's department for help. Suddenly, a clear, strong voice rang out above the tumult, singing a favorite hymn of the prisoners:

Yield not to temptation, for yielding is sin;
Each victory will help you, some other to win.
Fight manfully onward, dark passion subdue;
Look ever to Jesus, He'll carry you through.

There was a lull, then one after another joined in singing: "Yield not to temptation, for yielding is sin. . . ." And presently, with one accord, all formed into line, and marched quietly to their cells.

Time is short. Many are drifting away from God. They have yielded to sin and temptation in the worst forms. If there is no repentance, destruction is sure. But we have a mighty God who has promised: "If my people, which are called by my name, will humble themselves, and pray, and seek my face, and turn from their wicked ways, then will I hear from heaven, and forgive their sin, and will heal their land" (2 Chron. 7:14).

While the Saviour is speaking to your heart, will you

humble yourself, seek His face, and turn from your wicked ways? The Lord is waiting to forgive your sins the moment you turn to Him with all your heart.

Saviour, Like a Shepherd Lead Us!

Paddington Green is a postal designation and not, as one might assume, a pastel shade of color. The "Green" that was once a meadow is now only a small oval patch of green grass about fifty feet long.

I walked round the green in a vain search for an address. The old house has long since gone. There is a business building or shop there now. But I was not really looking for the shop; I was searching for a little lady who was born in 1799 and lived in that district most of her life. I was sorry that I missed her. I had so many questions I wanted to ask her. You see, I was looking for Dorothy Ann Thrupp, author of the beautiful hymn, "Saviour, Like a Shepherd Lead Us."

Dorothy Ann Thrupp was born at Paddington Green on June 20, 1799, and died near the place of her birth on December 14, 1847. Now I have no love for cold facts like that. The official records give the date of birth and death, but there those records end. Dorothy Ann Thrupp still lives in Paddington. She lives in the heart of the Shepherd she so dearly loved and served so faithfully. How beautifully she portrays her Saviour. We can just see Him as we sing her hymn, and to see Him is to love Him as Mrs. Thrupp did.

> Saviour, like a Shepherd lead us,
>   Much we need Thy tender care;
> In Thy pleasant pastures feed us,
>   For our use Thy folds prepare:

Blessed Jesus, Blessed Jesus,
    Thou hast bought us, Thine we are;
Blessed Jesus, Blessed Jesus,
    Thou hast bought us, Thine we are.

Never were the people of this world in greater need of Someone to guide them than they are today. Darkness seems to cover the earth, and gross darkness the people. We need light. We need a guide. There is only One who can help us. He is Jesus. He is the Light of the world. He is the Saviour, your Saviour, if you will trust Him. Our hearts go out to the people of Africa and Asia in their distress, their disillusionment, and their utter hopelessness and frustration. How they need the Saviour, like a Shepherd to lead them. How much, how very much, they need His tender care. Political systems of the world cannot give them what they need most—the Saviour's tender care.

We are Thine; do Thou befriend us,
    Be the Guardian of our way;
Keep Thy flock, from sin defend us,
    Seek us when we go astray:
Blessed Jesus, Blessed Jesus,
    Hear, O hear, us when we pray;
Blessed Jesus, Blessed Jesus,
    Hear, O hear, us when we pray.

Godless nations are seeking the friendship of those backward and undeveloped nations of the world. Communism does not really want their friendship, but she wants the rich resources of Africa and Asia. In short, the goal of Communism is to rule the world. This they can never do. The kingdoms of Africa, Asia and the world are to be ruled by our Saviour Shepherd, King of Kings and Lord of Lords, Jesus Christ, the Hope of every nation.

In Africa and in Asia, millions are crying out for deliverance from sin. Millions go and wash in the Ganges, but, alas, their sins are not washed away. Millions come to death's door in terror, screaming for deliverance from those evil spirits they so greatly fear. Only

Jesus can deliver them from sin and the evil one. Only Jesus can deliver you. You may not be living in heathen darkness, but if you do not know Jesus as your Saviour you are in a worse condition than you know. You are in worse condition than a man in the last stages of cancer, who does not know he is dying. You are dying in sin, and soon it may be too late to pray. This is not to frighten you, but to introduce you to your Saviour, who is seeking the lost, who is seeking you. He will hear you, if you will pray to Him for deliverance from your sins. He can save and He alone, and He will.

A Life Saved by this Hymn

It was Christmas Eve, 1875. Ira Sankey, whose gospel in song had been the means of bringing many to Christ, was with friends travelling up the Delaware River by steamboat. There were many passengers on their way home for Christmas. Sankey was asked to sing a hymn. He had thought to sing a Christmas carol, but felt he should sing "Saviour, Like a Shepherd Lead Us." After his hymn was finished a passenger asked to speak with Sankey. "Did you serve in the Union Army?" he asked. Sankey replied that he had. "Can you remember whether you were doing picket duty on a moonlight night in 1862?" Sankey replied again that he was. "I, too, was on duty that night, serving in the Confederate Army. I saw you standing at your post and I raised my musket to take aim. At that instant you began to sing. It was the same hymn you sang here tonight. Those words stirred my heart. I thought of my God-fearing mother. She sang that hymn to me many times. She died when I was but a lad, and I turned from her Shepherd. That night I could not shoot you. My arms dropped limp at my side. Tonight your singing has stirred me with terrible conviction. Can you help me to find peace for my sin-sick soul?" Sankey put his arm around the man who had once been his enemy in war, and led him to his Saviour.

Will you let Him be your Saviour now? He has loved you, loves you still. Ask Him now to forgive your sins, and to hear you as you pray. He will. He has bought you with a great price, His own blood. He is seeking you now.

Gentle Jesus, Meek and Mild

I often wonder how many children pray every day. I wonder if they are aware of the fact that Jesus really hears them when they pray.

Here is a prayer from many years ago. It is really a children's hymn, written by Charles Wesley, the brother of John Wesley who founded the Methodist Church. Charles Wesley had many children of his own to whom he taught this prayer:

Gentle Jesus, meek and mild,
Look upon a little child,
Pity my simplicity,
Suffer me to come to Thee.

Fain would I to Thee be brought;
Blessed Lord, forbid it not;
In the kingdom of Thy grace
Give a little child a place.

("Fain" is an Old English word meaning "gladly.")

Many men and women of God have been converted when they were small. John and Charles Wesley's mother taught them about Jesus from babyhood, and this was a wonderful foundation on which to build their own Christian experiences in later life. Children who have Christian parents are greatly blessed of God. Those who do not have Christian homes can be a marvelous witness to their families. Many a mother or father has been converted because of a little child's prayer. Here is the story of one family.

I learned, while living in England, about Joe King who lived in Yorkshire in the North of England. His story was written up in a Scottish magazine. He had a Christian wife and a little daughter of six years. He drank so much that he spent very little time at home.

One evening Mr. King came home from work earlier than usual, and, strangely enough, he had *not* been drinking. He came in the front door just as his wife was taking their little daughter up to bed. As he waited, he listened to them talking. When it came time for little Anne to pray, the first part of her prayer was the hymn we have quoted above. Then she added, "Jesus, save my dear, dear daddy." Her mother, who was evidently weeping, added with a sob in her throat, "Dear Lord, answer prayer."

That prayer of his little girl was too much for Joe to ignore. He went out into the dark street and began to think about what a wicked man he had been. He had whipped his little girl many times when he was drunk; she had been terribly afraid of him. Now, ashamed of himself, he wondered how he could ever have been so cruel to such a dear little girl, and now she who had never known a father's prayer or love could so lovingly pray for him! Standing there in the cold night air, with tears streaming down his cheeks, he prayed, "Lord, I am a wicked man. I am ashamed of the life I have lived. Answer my little girl's prayer and her mother's."

Then the light that never shone on land or sea shone into his heart. He went into the house a different man. Imagine how much rejoicing there was as he told his wife, who suffered so long, how God had answered prayer for him and changed his heart.

John B. Gough used to tell this true story: A friend of his was visiting homes in a poor district, trying to find people he could help with food and clothing. The door was open in one house, and, seeing a ladder extending up to an attic, he called. Receiving no answer, he climbed the ladder. A sad sight met his eyes: on a bed of sawdust lay a thin, sick-looking boy. What little clothes he had on were rags.

"What are you doing here?" he asked the child.

"Hush; don't tell anybody, please, sir."

"Where's your mother?"

"Mother is dead."

The little fellow then showed the man his back. There were big sores where blood had clotted and dried.

"Who beat you like that?" inquired the man.

"Father did, sir, because I won't steal anymore. He gets drunk and wants me to steal for him. But I won't steal anymore; so he whips me."

"Who told you not to steal?"

"I went to the Mission Sunday School and they told me about Jesus and His love; they told me about the commandment, 'Thou shalt not steal'—and I'll never steal again, even if my daddy kills me."

The good man nodded his head and said, "My dear boy, you cannot stay here. I will contact a kind lady who may be able to take care of you, and then I will come in a little while and get you."

"Thank you sir," said the little boy, "but before you go, would you like to hear me sing?" He raised up on his elbow and sang "Gentle Jesus, Meek and Mild." After he had sung the hymn through, he added, "That's the hymn I learned at Sunday School."

This good Samaritan prepared a room for the little boy and returned to get him. But another Friend had been there first. The starved little body was there, but the brave little spirit had gone to be with his new Friend, "Gentle Jesus, meek and mild."